Joomla! 2.5
Beginner's Guide!

written by Hagen Graf,
Jen Kramer, Milena Mitova, Angie Radtke, Henk van Cann

Joomla! 2.5
Beginner's Guide

Joomla! 2.5 - Beginner's Guide

About the Book 5

Introduction 8

Showcase 15

Installation 25

Structures and Terms 38

What's New? 47

Managing Content 55

Statuses, Trash and Check-Ins 80

Structure Your Content with Categories 84

Website and Content Configuration 91

Templates 97

Navigation 104

Users and Permissions 112

Extension Management 122

Core Extensions 126

Modules 149

Plug-Ins 152

Working with Templates 162

- The Beez Template 171
- Why SEO is important for you 184
- Multi-Language Websites 192
- A Joomla 2.5 Website from Scratch 201
- Upgrade from older versions 205
- Earning respect and money with Joomla 209
- Resources 221
- cocoate.com 223

Joomla! 2.5 - Beginner's Guide

About the Book

This book, as every book, has chapters, an outline, many screenshots and it covers the newest technology available in the "Joomlaverse".

It is based on the successful Joomla 1.6 and 1.7 - Beginner's Guide and has been extended with more chapters. All the existing chapters are reworked and new screenshots were taken, where it was necessary.

It is useful for readers, advertisers, authors, translators and of course the Joomla community because:

IT IS FREE OF CHARGE

It is free of charge readable on our website and downloadable as PDF

IT HELPS YOU TO SOLVE YOUR TASKS

There's a lot in the book to discover!

IT IS SPONSORED

The book is sponsored by various companies who are an important part of the Joomla community.

Thank you: PopcliQ, JoomlaShine, CloudAccess, VMX Pro / VM Expert, Digitalflo, SourceCoast, descartes, stackideas, savvy panda, redCOMPONENT, raramuri design, Joomlashack, iJoomer, Sigsiu.NET GmbH, JoomlaShowroom.com, tec-promotion, ARC Technology Group, iMaqma, Rochen, websites4u, Joomla Direct, PatVB, JoomlArt, Abivia, TechJoomla

It is still possible to sponsor the work and advertise in the book[1]

IT'S COLLABORATIVE WORK

Four additional authors besides me wrote chapters!

Thank you:

Milena Mitova[2] - Why SEO is important for you

Angie Radtke[3]. Chapter: The Beez Template

Henk van Cann[4]. Chapter: Earning respect and money with Joomla

---

[1] http://cocoate.com/j25/ad

[2] http://twitter.com/completewebcare

[3] http://www.der-auftritt.de/

[4] http://www.2value.nl/

Jen Kramer[5]. Chapter: A Joomla 2.5 Website from Scratch

It's multilingual

The book will be available in three more languages.

Spanish - Joomla 2.5 - Guía para principiantes

Thanks a lot to the translator Isidro Baquera (Gnumla)

Thanks a lot to the sponsor
Complusoft

Italian - Joomla 2.5 - Guida per Principanti

Thanks a lot to the translator Cinzia[6]

It is still possible to sponsor the work and advertise in the book[7].

Thanks a lot to the sponsors Sigsiu.NET, joomla.it,

German - Joomla 2.5 - Ein Anfängerbuch

Translator is me (Hagen Graf)

Thanks a lot to the sponsors Sigsiu.NET, digitalflo, tec-promotion, websites4u.ch, schwarzkünstler, CloudAccess

It is still possible to sponsor the work and advertise in the book[8].

French - Joomla 2.5 - Le Guide Pour Débutant

Thanks a lot to the translators Serge Billon[9] and Simon Grange[10]

Thanks a lot to the sponsors Sigsiu.NET, CloudAccess.

It is still possible to sponsor the work and advertise in the book[11].

---

[5] http://www.joomla4web.com/

[6] http://cocoate.com/cinzia

[7] http://cocoate.com/it/j25it/ad

[8] http://cocoate.com/de/j25de/ad

[9] http://cocoate.com/serge-billon

[10] http://cocoate.com/simon-grange

[11] http://cocoate.com/fr/j25fr/ad

Russian - Руководство для начинающего пользователя Joomla 2.5

Thanks a lot to the translator Alexey Baskinov[12]

Thanks a lot to the sponsor Sigsiu.NET, JoomlaArt

It is still possible to sponsor the work and advertise in the book[13].

Danish - Joomla 2.5 - Begynder Guide

Thanks a lot to the translator Ole Bang Ottosen[14]

It is still possible to sponsor the work and advertise in the book[15].

We want your feedback!

Comment on the chapters in the HTML versions and provide feedback.

Get involved in the next project!

The next Joomla Version is around the corner.

Join us!

---

[12] http://cocoate.com/ru/alexey-baskinov

[13] http://cocoate.com/ru/j25ru/ad

[14] http://cocoate.com/da/ole-bang-ottosen

[15] http://cocoate.com/da/j25da/ad

Joomla! 2.5 - Beginner's Guide

Chapter 1

Introduction

Welcome to Joomla. It is a free system for creating websites. It is an open source project, which, like most open source projects, is constantly in motion. It is unpredictable, sometimes indescribable, partially controversial, quite often very sexy and, at times, a little sleepy and provincial. Nevertheless, or perhaps because of these reasons, it has been extremely successful for six years now and is popular with millions of users worldwide.

Concerning the question whether to write Joomla (with a !) or Joomla (without a !) after years of finding out people reached a consensus:

> Use it once in the first instance of Joomla and then forget it!

The word Joomla is a derivative of the word Jumla from the African language of Swahili and means "all together".

The Project Joomla is the result of a heated discussion between the Mambo Foundation, which was founded in August 2005, and its then-development team. Joomla is a development of the successful system Mambo. Joomla is used all over the world for simple homepages and for complex corporate websites as well. It is easy to install, easy to manage and very reliable.

The Joomla team has organised and reorganised itself throughout the last six years

- From 2005 to 2009, Joomla 1.0 was further developed up to version 1.0.15 and that development was officially laid off in September 2009.

- From 2005 until now, Joomla 1.5 is still being developed, was introduced as a stable version in January 2008, and will officially 'end of life' (EOL) in April 2012.

- From 2008 until 2011, Joomla 1.6 was developed. A stable version has been available since January 2011.

- In July 2011 Joomla 1.7 was released

- Joomla 2.5 is the first long term release (LTS) since Joomla 1.5 was released in January 2012 (coming soon :))

The users of the Joomla system remained faithful. Many transferred their websites from Mambo to Joomla and they have learned a lot over the years.
Many users have climbed aboard in the last few years but there are still people in the world who do not

know about the system. Joomla, together with Drupal and WordPress, are the most used open source web content management system in the world.

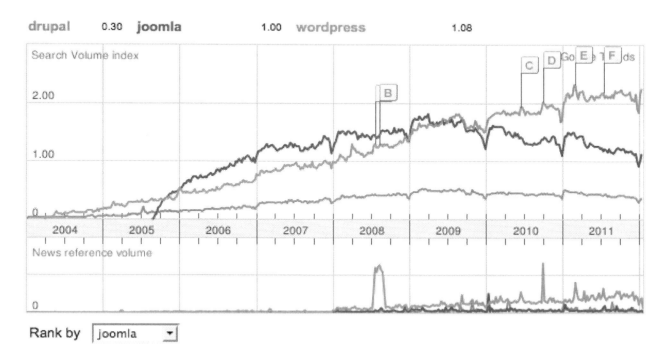

Figure 1: Google Trend 2012-01-17 worldwide Drupal, Joomla, WordPress

In *Figure 1*, Joomla and WordPress are on the same avarage level according to Google search volume trend. Joomla and Wordpress are searched three times as often as Drupal. However, the search volume for Joomla has been declining since 2010. It was time for Joomla to start rethinking with the release of the Joomla 1.6 version in January 2011 and Joomla 1.7 in July 2011.

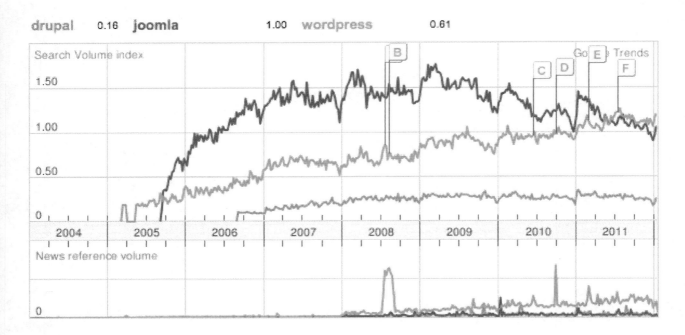

Figure 2: Google Trend 2012-01-17 Germany - Drupal, Joomla, WordPress

Compared to the world average, the situation in e.g. Germany is different (*Figure 2*). Joomla has almost twice as large of a search volume as WordPress and WordPress almost four times as much as Drupal.

Here are a few statistics from Google Trends (*Table 1*):

Country	Drupal	Joomla	WordPress
World	0.3	1	1.08
Chile	0	1	0.82
France	0.2	1	0.68
Germany	0.16	1	0.61
Italy	0.17	1	0.6
Poland	0.15	1	0.43
Russian Federation	0.3	1	0.5
Spain	0.26	1	1
Switzerland	0.15	1	0.45

UK	0.4	1	1.65
USA	0.66	1	2.3
China	0.8	1	3.2

Table 1 Google Trend - Drupal, Joomla, WordPress

There are significant national differences in the use of content management systems. In Germany, for example, the CMS TYPO3 also plays a role. The search volume is comparable to Joomla.

In January 2012, 2.8 % of the entire web is powered by Joomla[16]

The range of Joomla websites goes from very simple homepages to complex business applications and projects based on the Joomla Framework. What makes Joomla so successful, and the ways in which you can use it, will be described in this book.

WHO AM I?

My name is Hagen Graf, I'm 47 years old, and I live in *Fitou*[17], France. I am married to the woman of my dreams and have four daughters.

My work consists of many different activities such as teaching, advising, listening, testing, programming, understanding structures, developing new applications, questioning, and always trying something new.

Actually, my work can be done completely online but sometimes clients may have reservations about fully online projects, which is why I am on the road a lot. Being on the road means meeting clients in different countries with different languages and cultures, long car, bus or train rides as well as very short response times to customer enquiries, Facebook messages and tweets.

This way of working has implications for what I once used to call "the office".
I need to be able to have access from anywhere in the world to my e-mails, pictures, videos, tweets, and documents. My office is located where I am.

WHO ARE YOU?

Of course I do not know exactly what you do, but many people whom I have worked with work in a way similar to myself. Employees of larger companies however, for various reasons, often cannot or may not work as flexibly. Your own experience with computers is probably similar to mine. Many of us started with an older PC and a Windows system at school or at home, and then got to know from experience the

---

[16] w3techs.com/technologies/overview/content_management/all

[17] http://goo.gl/maps/3dU6

harsh reality of office applications, data loss, insufficient memory, and hard drive and printer configuration adventures. The wonderful relationships between these things have been changed with the user-centred way of Web 2.0 and the use of smart phones, but this does not necessarily make it easier.

If you do not love messing with passion at night with your operating system or telephone or sorting your photos and music, and moving them all from one device to another, then you are probably just like me - happy when your devices and applications are working, when you can access your data on the Internet and all is working smoothly. If you work from a home office, a smooth work environment becomes particularly important. Non-functioning soft- and hardware can quickly turn your situation into a nightmare.

I distinguish between the following types of users:

- **Visitors:** They visit a website and they do not care much about the system you used for creating the site.
- **Users:** They use the website. They create content using pre-defined procedures.
- Website Designers or Integrators: They install a Joomla site on a server, create categories, content, links and menu modules, configure templates and languages, are all-rounders and usually have the sole responsibility for the website.
- **CSS Designers:** They often like to work exclusively with files that have the extension *.css*.
- **HTML Designers:** They give CSS Designers the foundation they need for their work. In Joomla, they create the so-called template overrides.
- **Developers:** They know the programming languages PHP and JavaScript and like to use them. They enhance the Joomla core with additional functions.
- **Architects:** They think about security, speed and code quality.

The website designer plays a special role in this list. He usually has to cover all other roles, which constitutes a real challenge. As I am writing this book, I often find myself thinking about the website designer.

A company, an institution, a club, an organization, yes, probably everyone, needs a web presence that is user-friendly and flexible. A presence - one that develops over time, can easily be changed via a web browser. This presence can replace your filing cabinet and leather address book; this presence can communicate with different devices and it can be extended easily.

I assume your website already explains what you do or what your company does. This is your place where you maintain your customer relations 24 hours per day, seven days a week.
Your website probably contains a collection of applications and data summarising your activities. Your site should also contain interfaces to allow other applications to use them.

Until a few years ago, the creation of a website was a difficult thing to do. Whilst you did not have to be a renowned specialist, a combination of perseverance and having fun with what you are doing were necessary to produce appealing results. You had to create static HTML pages in an HTML editor and then upload them via file transfer protocol to a server. To create even the simplest interactivity such as a contact form or a forum, you had to learn a programming language.

It is more than understandable that many people did not take this hardship on themselves and handed over the creation of a website to a web agency or did not even start the project in the first place.

Thanks to Facebook and kits such as Google Sites, creating simple web pages has become relatively easy but if you want something unique, you should become familiar with a content management system.

Joomla offers everything you need to create your own, individual website.

WHAT IS THIS BOOK ABOUT?

First of all, it is about Joomla and how to use it.

Joomla is a tool with lots of possibilities and you can use the system in a huge variety of configurations, depending on your ideas and wishes.

In order to allow comfortable access, I have structured the book as follows:

1. This Introduction
2. Showcase
3. Installation
4. Structures and Terms
5. What's New?
6. Managing Content
7. How to Create an 'About Us' Page
8. A Typical Article
9. Media Manager
10. Contact Form
11. Status, Trash and Check Ins
12. Structure Your Content with Categories
13. Website and Content Configuration
14. Templates
15. Navigation

16. Users and Permissions

17. Extension Management

18. Core Extensions

19. Modules

20. Plug-Ins

21. Working with Templates

22. The Beez Template

23. Why SEO is important to you

24. Multi-Language Websites

25. A Joomla Website from Scratch

26. Upgrade from Older Versions

27. Earning respect and Money with Joomla

28. Resources?

Although you are a beginner, you will be able to manage your own Joomla website via a web browser. If you are somewhat familiar with HTML, CSS and image editing, you will be able to customize a template for your website.

ANY FURTHER QUESTIONS?

Don't hesitate![18] Of course, I can't deliver technical support. The Joomla forums provide a wealth of knowledge and you will definitely find answers to your questions there. If you have comments or questions about the book, however, please feel free to leave them in the comments section below.

---

[18] http://cocoate.com/j25

Chapter 2

Showcase

What do websites look like when they were created with Joomla?

This question can't be answered easily as most websites are based on the Joomla software, but the design is created by an agency and then "transformed" into a Joomla template. Therefore, the exterior of a website can be deceiving. Nevertheless, here are some screenshots to give you an idea.

ALLIANCE FOR CATHOLIC EDUCATION - UNIVERSITY OF NOTRE DAME

The Alliance for Catholic Education, or ACE, uses Joomla 1.7 to manage their multifaceted web presence. ACE is a collaborative effort of twelve different programs all working to strengthen and sustain Catholic schools in the United States. Joomla, along with the Gantry template framework, allows ACE to maintain twelve unique sites in one through the use of Joomla and Gantry's multiple template options (eg: http://ace.nd.edu/teach is a unique homepage for one of the programs within the site). All of ACE's units build off the same Joomla instance and database, maintain a strong visual connection to the main homepage and also share the same features for all members of the organization including: an integrated news feed, online membership, a JomSocial Network, several blogs, a job-board and an online catalogue of publications.

Some of ACE's favorite extensions are: Yootheme's Zoo, Sh404sef, JCE, JSPT and Socialable's Autogroup.

Future plans involve integrating a CRM (CiviCRM) to function within the Joomla framework. (*Figure 1*)!

Joomla! 2.5 - Beginner's Guide

Figure 1: University of Notre Dame

Website: ace.nd.edu

Creator: CloudAccess.net, Ricky Austin[19]

3000+ Government Websites built with Joomla

JoomlaGov is a showcase for Government sites powered by Joomla around the world. More than 200 countries are represented and, one month after its launch at 'J and Beyond' 2011, it contains more than 3,000 sites.

---

[19] http://ace.nd.edu/directory/ricky-austin

This site is a great example of how the Joomla community[20] can collaborate, to highlight the qualities of the Joomla CMS. FFor instance, the Citizen Portal of the Federal District Government Mexico City, Mexiko[21] is well worth a look. (*Figure 3*).

Figure 3: JoomlaGov

Website built using Joomla, K2 & Google Maps (API version 3). The video was recorded at Joomla Day South Africa 2011. Case Study - How we built the joomlagov.info Website - Dwight Barnard (ZA)[22]

Website: www.joomlagov.info

Creator: raramuridesign & piezoworks.be

THE EIFFEL TOWER

Well, probably you know this building (*Figure 4*)!

---

[20] http://joomlagov.info/about

[21] http://www.df.gob.mx/

[22] http://vimeo.com/32790888

Figure 4: The Eiffel Tower

Well, probably you know this building!

Website: tour-eiffel.fr

Creator: Mairie de Paris (paris.fr)

eCommerce

A danish online shop based on Joomla and the RedShop component (*Figure 5*).

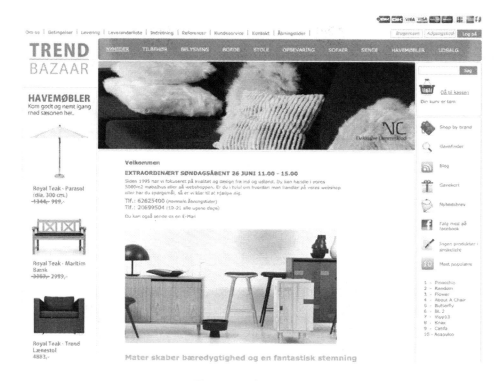

Figure 5: Trend Bazaar

Website built using Joomla, K2 & Google Maps (API version 3)

Website: www.trendbazaar.dk

Creator: redweb.dk

KOKORO

Kokoro stands for: chocolate that comes from the heart and soul. (*Figure 6*).

Figure 6: Kokoro

Website built using Joomla, K2 & Google Maps (API version 3)

Website: kokorochocolate.com

Creator: ohappens.nl

TRANQUILLITY BLUE

Tranquillity Blue is a site to showcase activites and adventures in a small coastal town on the South West Coast of Africa. The aim was to make the site manageable by the client and flexible enough to grow and encompass advanced functionality if needed. (*Figure 7*).

Figure 7: Tranquillity Blue

Website: www.tranquillityblue.co.za

Agency: raramuridesign.com

Design: Dwight Barnard

AND?

These websites look how websites are supposed to look. :-)
If I had not told you that they were created with Joomla, you probably would not have noticed it consciously.

More examples can be found in an article from January 2012 in techrepublic: 15 Joomla implementations[23]

HOW TO FIND JOOMLA SITES?

I will show a few ways to find websites made with Joomla.

---

[23] http://www.techrepublic.com/blog/webmaster/inspiration-15-joomla-implementations/1085

joomla.org

Just have a look at the project site! I found the sites featured above in the Joomla Showcase [24]. You will find 2,000 websites sorted by category. There is a site of the month, an overview with top-rated sites, and much more (*Figure 8*).

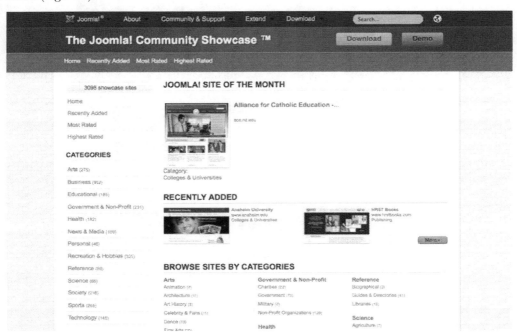

Figure 8: Joomla Showcase

Google

You can search for the term com_content[25]. The component "content" uses this term in the URL of the page. Nowadays, this kind of searching is not really effective because of the various search engine optimized URLs' but the result is still impressive.

WAPPALYZER FIREFOX EXTENSION

Wappalyzer[26] is a browser extension (Firefox) that identifies software on websites (*Figure 10*).

---

[24] http://community.joomla.org/showcase/

[25] http://www.google.de/search?q=com_content

[26] https://addons.mozilla.org/en-US/firefox/addon/wappalyzer/

Figure 9: Wappalyzer

CHECK OUT THE WEBSITE MORE CLOSELY

If you are on a website and want to know whether it was created with Joomla, have a look at the source code. In the header section, you should find this line:

```
<meta name="generator" content="Joomla - Open Source
Content Management" />
```

You can also just type the URL of the link to the administration area:

```
http://example.com/administrator
```

Here the example of the Eiffel tower site: [27]:

---

[27] http://www.tour-eiffel.fr/administrator/

Administration of the Eiffel tower website

GO AHEAD AND ASK YOUR FRIENDS

I tweeted

```
I want YOUR site :) Looking for 5+ great Joomla site
examples for the showcase chapter cocoate.com/j25/
showcase plz reply a link+RT
```

and promand promptly received the links for the sites you can see above!

ANY OTHER IDEAS?

Do you know any other ways to of detecting Joomla sites? Feel free to leave comments[28].

---

[28] http://cocoate.com/node/10292

Joomla! 2.5 - Beginner's Guide

Chapter 3

Installation

Thanks to the web installer, Joomla can be installed in only a few minutes.

In order to install Joomla on your local PC, it is necessary to set up your "own internet", for which you'll need a browser, a web server, a PHP environment and as well a Joomla supported database system. We call this a LAMP stack[29] (or XAMP) and a client server system. The Joomla files will be copied to this system and configured with the Joomla web installer.

MINIMUM SYSTEM REQUIREMENTS:

- an installed and functioning web server, like Apache (with mod_mysql, mod_xml, and mod_zlib), version 2.x or Microsoft IIS 7.
- the PHP scripting language, version 5.2.4.
- the MySQL database system, version 5.0.4.

INSTALLATION VARIANTS

You need all the components mentioned above to install a Joomla system for yourself. PC, browser, and Internet connection are usually available. There are a number of options for web server, PHP interpreter, and database. You can:

- set the system up locally on your PC
- set the system up on a server in a company's Intranet
- rent a virtual server from a provider
- rent or purchase a server from a provider (with root access)

You can also have the web server and database located on computers that are physically separated from each other.

You can also, of course, use different:

- brands of web servers
- Versions of PHP interpreters

---

[29] http://en.wikipedia.org/wiki/LAMP_%28software_bundle%29

- Versions of MySQL databases

And on top of that, you can install and operate all these components on various operating systems.

This freedom in choice of resources can sometimes confuse a layman. Therefore, we will discuss a few typical scenarios.

Local Test Environment

If you are at home or in your office, for example, and want to set up a Joomla website, you may use any of the following operating systems.

Windows Operating System

For a Windows operating system you can use either of two web servers:.

You take a pre-configured package (XAMPP), unpack it on your computer, and everything you need is there (http://apachefriends.org).

Linux Operating System

Here it depends on the distribution version you have. All the distributions allow simple installation (with a click of the mouse) of the Apache, PHP, and MySQL packages. At times, depending on distribution, they may already be pre-installed. So you can use the programs contained in the distribution or a preconfigured package (XAMPP); extract it on your computer and everything you need is there (http://apachefriends.org).

Mac OS X Operating System

In Mac OS X operating system, you have a default web server (Apache) in your system that you have to activate, but unfortunately not PHP and no MySQL.

So you can use the installed Apache web server and install the missing software or the pre-configured XAMPP package for Mac OS X. Another complete package by the name of MAMP is also very popular with the Mac OS X environment (http://www.mamp.info).

Production Environment

You have several options here as well.

Rented Virtual Server

You rent a web-space package with database, PHP support, and often also your domain name from a provider. In this case you have a functional environment and you can install your Joomla into it. Consult your provider as to the version choices (PHP, MySQL). Sometimes providers offer Joomla pre-installed with various templates. IIf this is the case, all you have to do is activate Joomla with a click of the mouse and it is ready for you.

Your Own Server

You rent a server from a provider and install the operating system of your choice. You are the administrator of the system and you can work on it, just like on your PC at home.

Before you venture into the wilderness of the Internet, you should first practice on your local computer. This has the advantage that there are no connection fees, it is very fast, and you can practice at a leisurely pace.

You may even have a small local network at home where you can install Joomla on one computer and access it from another.

Remember that there are probably more current versions on the respective project sites on the Internet.

Stumbling stones

This topic is very complex because there is a vast number of providers and an even greater number of installed web server, PHP, MySQL versions and web space management tools. Crunchpoints during the installation often consist of:

- an activated PHP Safe Mode, preventing you to upload files,
- 'forbidden' rewrite paths with the Apache web server because the so-called Apache Rewrite Engine (mod_rewrite) is not activated,
- the directory permissions on Linux and OSX, which are set differently than in Windows.

Basically, the easiest way that almost always works, is the following:

- Download the current file package from joomla.org to your home PC and unzip everything into a temporary directory.
- Load the unpacked files via FTP onto your rented server or to the directory of your local installation. The files must be installed in the public directory. These directories are usually called *htdocs*, *public_html* or *html*. If there already are other installations in that directory, you can specify a sub directory in which your Joomla files should be installed. Many web hosts allows you to link your rented domain name to a directory.
- You have to find out the name of your database. In most cases, one or more databases are included in your web hosting package. Sometimes, the names of the user, database and password are already given; sometimes you have to set them up first. Usually you can do this in a browser-based configuration interface. You will need the database access information for Joomla's web installer.

Joomla web installer

Download Joomla 2.5 at joomla.org[30] and unpack the files into your root folder of the web server (e.g.: /htdocs). From now on, everything is going to go really fast because the Joomla web installer is working for you. Go to URL *http://localhost/*.

Step 1 – Selecting a language

The web installer appears with a selection of languages. Choosing the language is the first of seven installation steps. Set the desired language, and click the Next button (*Figure 1*).

Figure 1: Installer – Select language

Step 2 – Installation check

The *Installation check* (*Figure 2*) should help you verify whether your server environment is suitable for the installation of Joomla or not.

---

[30] http://www.joomla.org/download.html

Joomla! 2.5 - Beginner's Guide

Figure 2: Installer – Installation check

It's a good sign if you see mostly green test results. Depending on your configuration, there can be differences. The Joomla Installer considers the configuration settings of the web server (in our case Apache), PHP, and the operating system. When using Unix Systems (Linux, Mac OS X), you have to pay attention to *file permissions*. This is particularly important for the file *configuration.php*. This file will be generated at the end of the installation with your personal values. If the installer can not write in the folder, Joomla can not create the file and the installation will fail. In this case, try to configure the rights and then click the button *repeat check*. Then, click the *Next* button and you will get to the step *license*.

Step 3 – License

Each software product is somehow licensed. Joomla is licensed according to the GNU General Public License, version 2.0 (*Figure 3*).

Joomla! 2.5 - Beginner's Guide

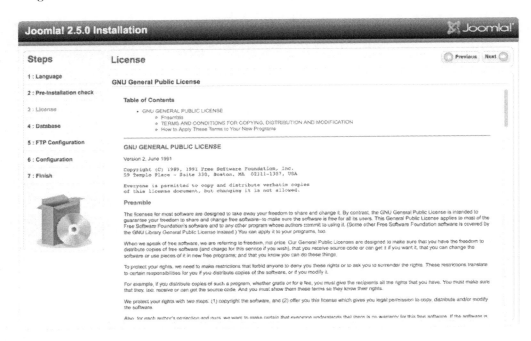

Figure 3: Installer – License

Step 4 – Database

In the fourth step *database configuration,* your data base parameters will be requested (*Figure 4*). You can create any number of databases in your local server environment. You have a MySQL user with the name *root*. The user root is the MySQL administrator and can, therefore, do everything in your MySQL system. The password depends on your server environment (no password is needed with XAMPP, with MAMP the password is root).

Joomla! 2.5 - Beginner's Guide

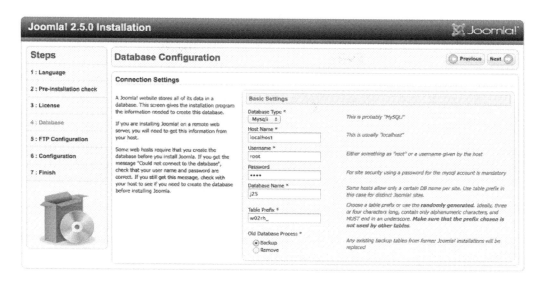

Figure 4: Installer – database configuration

Enter the following values into your local installation:

computer name: localhost

user name: root

password: [only you know that]

Now select the database name. In a productive environment on a database server with a provider, you probably have a fixed quota of databases and the database credentials are predefined. If you have root permission on your MySQL server, you can enter a name of a new database. Joomla will then create that database.

You can select whether the tables of any existing Joomla installation in this database should be cleared or saved and marked with the prefix bak_.

The *MySQL table prefix* is really practical. In front of each table name generated by the web installer, it writes the text that you typed in the appropriate field. As a default, the web installer suggests a randomly created one, like *w02rh_*. This has a simple reason. Sometimes you may only be able to get one MySQL database from your provider. If you want to run two or more Joomla sites, you have a problem, as the tables do not differ from each other. With the table prefix it is possible to distinguish several tables (*w01client_* or *w02client_*). Here, you should use the default *w02rh_* . The prefix is also used to indicate saved data (*bak_*); see above.

Step 5 - FTP-configuration

In order to avoid problems with access rights and possibly turned on PHP Safe Mode, you have the possibility to use the FTP functions of PHP for the upload and file handling. This is not necessary in a local installation. If you have installed Joomla on a virtual server with your provider, you can enter the FTP data provided by your ISP. If your provider allows this function, it is advisable for security reasons, to create different FTP accounts for users and for the Joomla installation. Activate the FTP account just for that Joomla directory (*Figure 5*).

Figure 5: Installer – FTP-configuration

Step 6 - Configuration

The main configuration is divided into three steps.

In the first part of the configuration the name of your site is requested. This name will appear in the title bar of the browser window when someone accesses your site. The name is also used at various other places, such as in confirmation emails to registered users. For our example page, I'll use the name Joomla (*Figure 6*). In the second part, the name, e-mail address and administrator password are requested. Writing down the password on a piece of paper is probably best (but do not stick it on the screen or under the keyboard :-)).

In the third part, you specify the type of data your Joomla installation should contain.

Installation of sample data

The data is the most important thing in your installation. Joomla allows (and strongly recommends for beginners) the installation of sample data. You will be provided with a small manual about Joomla and many examples to experiment safely. Click the button *install sample data*. The installer will load the data into your database and change the display (*Figure 6*). This process is somewhat unimpressive but necessary for installing sample data. The button will disappear and a small text box will be visible.

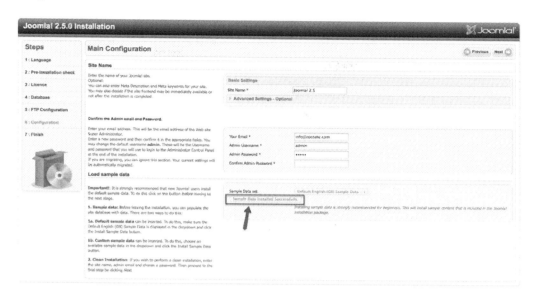

Figure 6: Installer – Configuration – Name, E-Mail, Password, Sample data

Click on the button *NEXT* and the data will be transferred.

Step 7 – Completion

In the seventh and final step you will be congratulated on having successfully installed Joomla (*Figure 7*). Congratulations from me as well! You will now see an advisory in bold letters appearing in the display, prompting you to delete the directory called 'Installation'. You should follow this advisory because your Joomla website will otherwise not run properly.

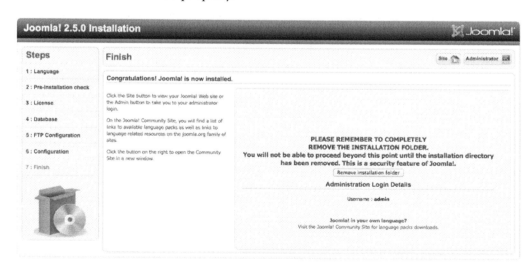

Figure 7: Installer – Completion

Joomla! 2.5 - Beginner's Guide

Note: A file named configuration.php has been created in your document directory. If you would like to repeat the installation, you will need to delete the file *configuration.php* before deleting the *installation directory*. The Joomla installer will start anew when you pull up the URL in your browser, where your Joomla files are located.

Now that you have fully installed Joomla you can begin configuring your website and content. You have the choice between the buttons *Site* (see website) and *Admin* (administration interface). Go ahead and have a look at your newly created website and click on *Site*. In case you have not yet deleted the *installation directory*, you will once again receive a friendly reminder to do so now and then refresh the page. The result looks very impressive (*Figure 8*).

Figure 8: Your website directly after installation

Have a look around, browse through a few options and try to familiarize yourself with your new site. Many features of Joomla are being used on this website filled with sampla data. Next, we are going to look at these in detail!

UNPUBLISH EXAMPLE DATA

If you are installing Joomla 2.5 for the first time, I recommend you also install the example data. Take your time and explore the website and how it all comes together. The example data show you how the website looks with content and comes with short explanations of the example content and modules. To get a brief overview, read the 50 pages behind the menu item "Using Joomla".

Now that you have seen enough, you would probably love to configure your website according to your needs and wishes.

How to get an empty Joomla ?

To get an empty version, you can:

- Install a fresh Joomla 2.5 without example data:
  Create a new folder in your local web directory (*/htdocs*) and install the new Joomla. Now you have two complete Joomla installations. This approach is very helpful for training purposes.

- Delete the example data in your administration area.

- Unpublish the example data. Please watch the video attached, in which I am going to show you how to do that.

If you decide to follow step 2 or 3, you will need to login in the administration area. There you can delete and/or unpublish the example data and menu items.

Menu manager

Go to the Menu Manager in the *Top Menu* (Menus -> Top), click the check boxes on the left side above the menu items to choose all of them, and then click the icon *Unpublish*. After you have done this, you will see a red icon on each menu item (*Figure 9*). If you now go back to your website (refresh it), you will notice that the top menu is no longer visible. Repeat the same procedure with the *Main Menu* and the *About Joomla* menu. Make sure you choose all menu items, except the Home/Frontpage item. This menu item cannot be deleted because you need a frontpage. In the lower area, you may change the number of displayed menu items (*Figure 10*).

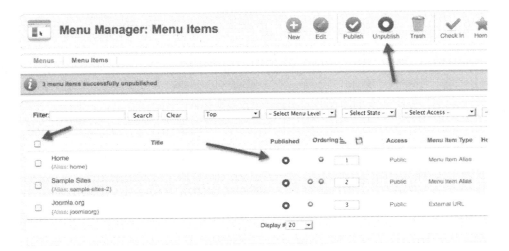

Figure 9: Menu manager I

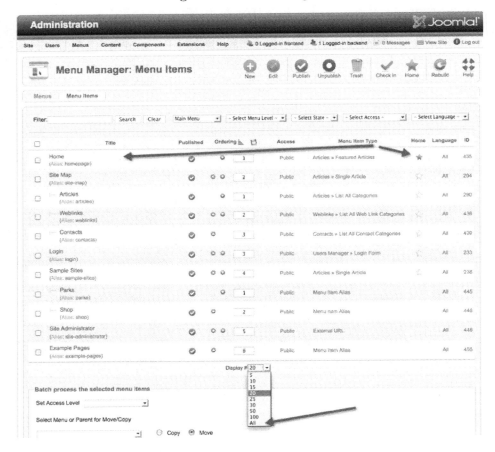

Figure 10: Menu manager II

Article manager

Use the same procedure as described above. Open the article manager and choose all content items to unpublish or delete them.

Cache

To make sure that all data will disappear from you site, you have to clear the entire cache (*Site Maintenance -> Clear Cache*). Again, choose all content and delete it.

Empty Website

Your Joomla is now "empty" (*Figure 11*).

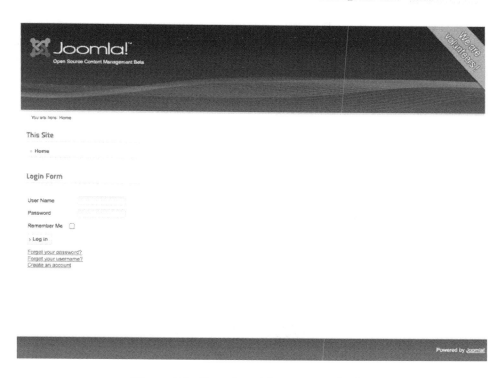

Figure 11: Joomla without example data

Chapter 4
Structures and Terms

I would like to explain and clarify some structures and terms before we begin with the configuration.

FRONTEND

With the frontend we mean the areas of the website as visitors or registered users see it. A registered user normally works only in the frontend. It is like in a store, where the goods are displayed in shop windows and on shelves. Here you can have a look around.

BACKEND

This is your administration area, therefore, we call it just administration. You can give registered users the right to work in your backend. This privilege is mostly limited to several employees, who should administer some tasks on the website. You can access the administration login via /administrator.
http://localhost/administrator
There you can register with your login details and choose your preferred language. (*Figure 1*).

Figure 1: Joomla Administration registration

Once logged in successfully, you'll have access to the administration, which is structured according to your user rights. (*Figure 2*).

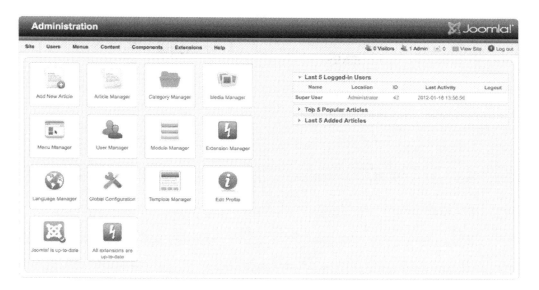

Figure 2: Administration

You may access each function either by using the combined menu tab system or by simply clicking an icon on the start screen.

FILES

Joomla consists of hundreds of files. Images, PHP scripts, CSS files, JavaScript files and a many more.

You probably already noticed this when you unpacked the compressed package and copied it into the htdocs folder. Basically, you have already installed two Joomla packages: one for the frontend and one for the backend. The 'Backend Joomla' is located in the *administrator* folder (*Figure 3*).

This folder is addressed when you call /administrator in the browser. Inside that folder are other folders like *cache*, *components*, *language*, *modules* and *templates*. The specific backend files are stored in these directories.

You will find the same folder names again outside the *administrator* folder. These folders contain the frontend files. These are not really two Joomla packages, but there is a clear separation between backend and frontend files.

For example, all files uploaded with the *Media Manager* will be saved in the */media* folder. All files have to be saved with a backup.

```
▼ 📁 administrator          Jan 11, 2012 6:27 PM    --        Folder
  ▶ 📁 cache                Jan 11, 2012 6:27 PM    --        Folder
  ▶ 📁 components           Jan 11, 2012 6:27 PM    --        Folder
  ▶ 📁 help                 Jan 11, 2012 6:27 PM    --        Folder
  ▶ 📁 includes             Jan 11, 2012 6:27 PM    --        Folder
    📄 index.php            May 31, 2011 1:10 AM    2 KB      TextW...ument
  ▶ 📁 language             Jan 11, 2012 6:27 PM    --        Folder
  ▶ 📁 manifests            Jan 11, 2012 6:27 PM    --        Folder
  ▶ 📁 modules              Jan 11, 2012 6:27 PM    --        Folder
  ▶ 📁 templates            Jan 11, 2012 6:27 PM    --        Folder
▶ 📁 cache                  Jan 11, 2012 6:27 PM    --        Folder
▶ 📁 cli                    Jan 11, 2012 6:27 PM    --        Folder
▶ 📁 components             Jan 11, 2012 6:27 PM    --        Folder
  📄 htaccess.txt           Apr 7, 2011 5:47 PM     3 KB      Plain Text
▶ 📁 images                 Jan 11, 2012 6:27 PM    --        Folder
▶ 📁 includes               Jan 11, 2012 6:27 PM    --        Folder
  📄 index.php              Feb 21, 2011 8:44 PM    1 KB      TextW...ument
▶ 📁 installation           Jan 11, 2012 6:27 PM    --        Folder
  📄 joomla.xml             Jan 11, 2012 6:27 PM    2 KB      TextW...ument
▶ 📁 language               Jan 11, 2012 6:27 PM    --        Folder
▶ 📁 libraries              Jan 11, 2012 6:27 PM    --        Folder
  📄 LICENSE.txt            Dec 12, 2009 4:44 PM    18 KB     Plain Text
▶ 📁 logs                   Jan 11, 2012 6:27 PM    --        Folder
▶ 📁 media                  Jan 11, 2012 6:27 PM    --        Folder
▶ 📁 modules                Jan 11, 2012 6:27 PM    --        Folder
▶ 📁 plugins                Jan 11, 2012 6:27 PM    --        Folder
  📄 README.txt             Sep 25, 2011 9:00 PM    4 KB      Plain Text
  📄 robots.txt             Sep 20, 2011 3:37 PM    865 bytes Plain Text
▶ 📁 templates              Jan 11, 2012 6:27 PM    --        Folder
▶ 📁 tmp                    Jan 11, 2012 6:27 PM    --        Folder
  📄 web.config.txt         Jan 10, 2012 7:26 PM    2 KB      Plain Text
```

Figure 3: Joomla 2.5 files and folder

DATABASE

Additionally to files (graphics, documents, system files, etc.) Joomla also needs a database. During the installation procedure, the Joomla web installer creates 61 tables in your specified database (*Figure 4*). In these tables, all content will be managed.

Joomla! 2.5 - Beginner's Guide

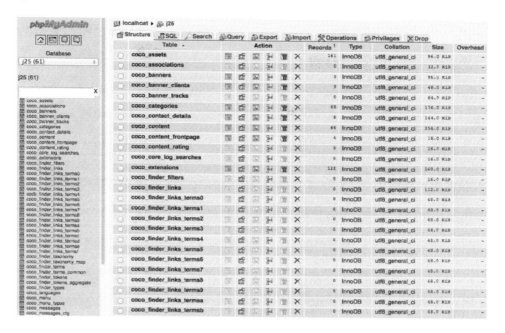

Figure 4: The Joomla data base tables

When I say content, I mean texts and configuration settings. The tables in the screenshot are displayed by means of phpMyAdmin. phpMyAdmin is a part of **XAMPP** and **MAMP** and is available via http://localhost/phpMyAdmin

Usually, no changes need to be made in these tables. In case you forget your admin password, phpMyAdmin is very helpful.

This software can also be used for backing up your database by creating a so-called SQL dump, as your tables have to be secured regularly.

ELEMENTS OF JOOMLA

The structure of Joomla is simple, sophisticated and efficient.
Joomla assumes that you want to write an article. An article usually consists of a title, text and some configuration settings.

Article

Articles can be displayed in single or list view. On the frontpage of your your recently installed Joomla website you will see these four articles (*Figure 5*).

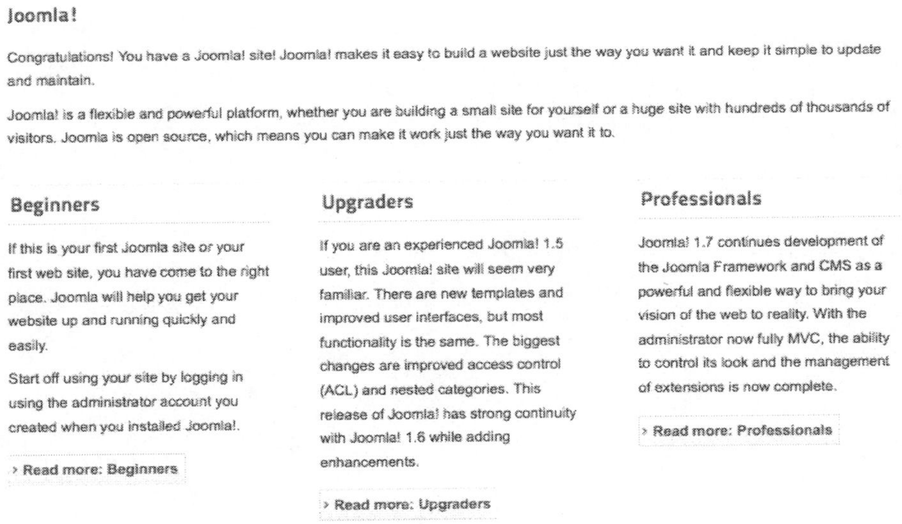

Figure 5: Article on frontpage

The articles are sorted in a certain manner. The first article is displayed by using the full width of the website. The other articles are placed below in three columns. If the articles are too long, you may insert a *read more* link. This representation is a list view. By clicking on the *read more* link you will be redirected to the single representation of that article (*Figure 6*). The type of display can be changed by setting *options* in the backend, however, only by the user with corresponding access rights.

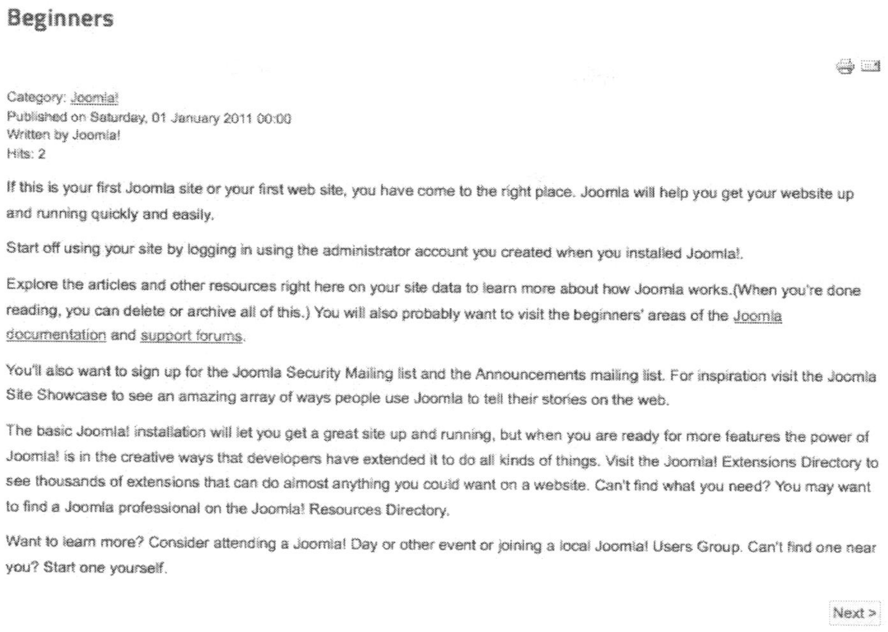

Beginners

Category: Joomla!
Published on Saturday, 01 January 2011 00:00
Written by Joomla!
Hits: 2

If this is your first Joomla site or your first web site, you have come to the right place. Joomla will help you get your website up and running quickly and easily.

Start off using your site by logging in using the administrator account you created when you installed Joomla!.

Explore the articles and other resources right here on your site data to learn more about how Joomla works.(When you're done reading, you can delete or archive all of this.) You will also probably want to visit the beginners' areas of the Joomla documentation and support forums.

You'll also want to sign up for the Joomla Security Mailing list and the Announcements mailing list. For inspiration visit the Joomla Site Showcase to see an amazing array of ways people use Joomla to tell their stories on the web.

The basic Joomla! installation will let you get a great site up and running, but when you are ready for more features the power of Joomla! is in the creative ways that developers have extended it to do all kinds of things. Visit the Joomla! Extensions Directory to see thousands of extensions that can do almost anything you could want on a website. Can't find what you need? You may want to find a Joomla professional on the Joomla! Resources Directory.

Want to learn more? Consider attending a Joomla! Day or other event or joining a local Joomla! Users Group. Can't find one near you? Start one yourself.

Next >

Figure 6: single display of an article

Articles can be published (*publish)* or not published (*unpublish*). You can feature articles on your frontpage, you can archive them or put them in the trash and retrieve them. You can copy and move them.

Categories

In order to display articles clearly, you must create categories, and then assign an article to them. Each article can be assigned to exactly one category (*Figure 7*). The categories can be nested to any depth. Articles from one or multiple categories can be assigned to one menu item and displayed in various ways. By clicking on the menu item, all articles from different categories will be shown. This principle is used by online newspapers, for example. You click on *Sports* and get all categorized articles for this topic. If the newspaper discerns between different forms of sports, they will use nested category trees:

- Sports
  - Football
  - Handball
- Politics
  - Domestic
  - Europe

- World

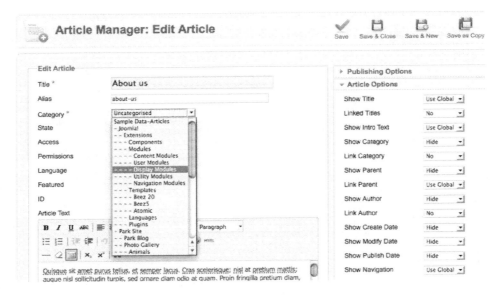

Figure 7: Category assignment

User

Users are needed to produce content. At least one user is registered on each Joomla site, namely the one you created during the installation, with the rights to configure everything on your site. Depending on the user's rights, he can work in frontend and/or backend to write an article. Each user requires a username, an email address and a password. Every user can be assigned to any user group as well as to any access level. This enables the user to create articles that are only visible to certain user groups.

Navigation

To find your way around the website, you will need navigation with corresponding links. In Joomla we call this a *menu*. You may create as many menus as desired and nest them into as many different ways as you wish. Each menu is a module which can be positioned on a provided area in the template.

Module

A module is something that you can position next to an article. A menu, for example, is a module. The small registration block on the left side is also a module. You can create as many modules with smart functions as you need and position them on the predefined area in the template.

Templates

A template is the graphical pattern for your website. It mostly consists of HTML and CSS files. Joomla delivers several templates for you to choose from. Templates are configurable, which allows you to upload a different logo, change the background color, etc. Each template provides areas where modules can be positioned (*Figure 8*).

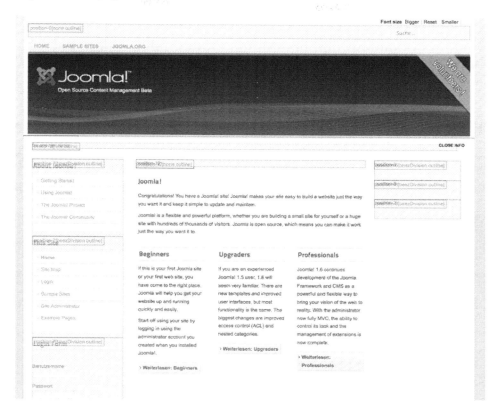

Figure 8: Template Positions

You can group modules around one or more articles.

Plug-ins

A plug-in provides practical services but is usually invisible to the visitors of the site. A wysiwyg editor, for example, is a plug-in. Plug-ins are extensions, which can be installed unlimited amount of times. The core package already consists of numerous useful plug-ins.

Components

Components are the little surprise packages that help you create nearly anything on your site. You want to have a booking system for workshops? A platform for properties? A forum? An image gallery? You just have to install the right component!
The Joomla core package already comes with some components, e.g., the contact component, which

enables you to integrate contact forms into your site. There are thousands of components to enhance your Joomla system.

Options

You will need individual configuration settings for your website; we call them options. These options are applied to the whole website, for users, categories, modules, components. You will always find an icon named *Options* like, e.g., that one (*Figure 9*), which provides you with the possibility to see the position of modules (*Figure 8*) by inserting *http://localhost/index.php?tp=1*
The initial *tp* stands for template position.

Figure 9: Options

Other structures

Other structures for user interfaces, templates and technical relations are also available. For the time being, you are well equipped by remembering the described structures above.

Chapter 5

What's New?

Joomla 2.5 will be released in January 2012 and it is the successor of Joomla 1.5. It will be a so called long term release and it will be the Joomla state of the art until July 2013. The versions 1.6 and 1.7 were short term releases and they paved the way to Joomla 2.5.

When you already upgraded your site from Joomla 1.5 to Joomla 1.7 in 2011 you probably use all the new features introduced with Joomla 1.6 and 1.7. When you scroll down and read the list of new features compared to Joomla 1.5 then you realize that 2011 was a very interesting year for Joomla.

But let's have a closer look at the new features for Joomla 2.5.

NEW FEATURES IN JOOMLA 2.5

The shiny new Joomla Platform

The Joomla Platform Version 11.4 is now the base of the CMS.
That means many more possibilities for third party developers e.g. image manipulation with the JImage class and generation of HTML tables with the JGrid class. A new version of the JavaScript library MooTools is used (1.4). If you don't know what Joomla platform is about, read Write your own App using Joomla Platform[31] and the official announcement of the Joomla Platform release[32].

Find more content with Smart Search

Search is "reinvented" in Joomla 2.5 with Finder. The new finder component works with a search index (*Figure 1*).

---

[31] http://cocoate.com/node/9582

[32] http://developer.joomla.org/news/378-version-11-3-of-the-joomla-platform-released.html

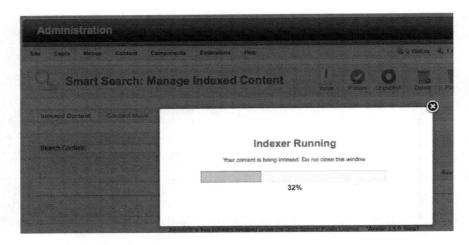

Figure 1: Creating the search index

Finder pre-searches your content. Search results are scored dynamically based on the context and frequency of search terms. The most relevant content will always be listed at the top of the results. It suggests alternative phrases (*Figure 2*) and its pluggable adapter system allows to install new search adapters which provide support for standard Joomla content and many other types of documents. Custom search filters allows you to provide contextual searching when your visitor is looking at particular sections of your Web site.

Figure 2: Suggestions

Spread Joomla to more Platforms by using more Databases

With Joomla 2.5 it will be possible to run Joomla on MySQL and Microsoft SQL Server and Microsoft Azure. Drivers for PostgreSQL and Oracle seems to be very near (Getting Ready for Multi-Database Support[33]).

Better Choices for Offline Mode

You can use the default offline message, disable it or create a customized message. Additionally you can select an image for the offline mode page (*Figure 3*). You even have a possibility to set the site to offline mode during installation so no unauthorized people can see it before you want them to.

---

[33] http://community.joomla.org/blogs/community/1526-getting-ready-for-muti.html

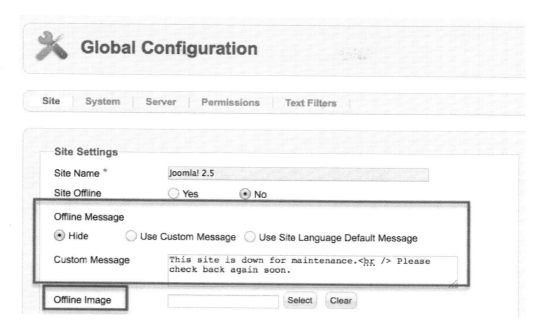

Figure 3: Offline mode options

User registrations with Captcha

A Captcha plugin using the reCAPTCHA service[34] can be enabled (*Figure 4*). Once you sign up for free with reCAPTCHA and enter your keys, you can enable Captcha on new user registrations. It could also be used by other extensions needing Captcha.

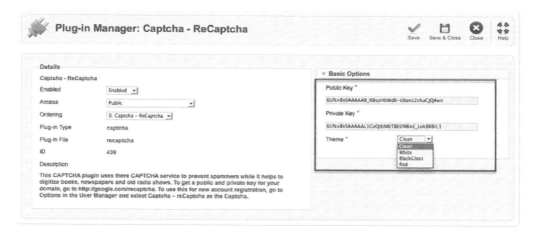

Figure 4: Captcha

---

[34] http://www.google.com/recaptcha

Easier handling for simple Layouts

You can now attach an image for the intro text to use in blog and featured layouts, an image for the full article text and up to three links for the full article layout. This means that your content creators won't have to fuss about an image in the text and your article format will be cleaner and more consistent.

MULTILANGUAGE

You can override the default language strings in a new manager in the backend (*Figure 5*).

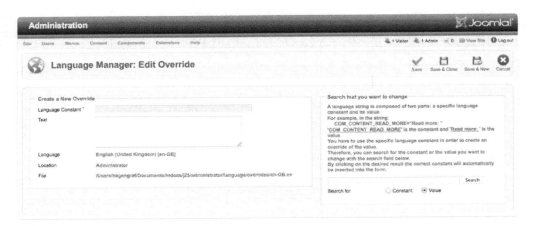

Figure 5:Language overrides manager

User Notes

A new feature "User Notes" allows to create notes attached to specific user accounts. Creating a user note you can also set a date which can be used later, for example, for user-related tasks organizing. You can have multiple notes per user and the notes can be in different categories (*Figure 6*).

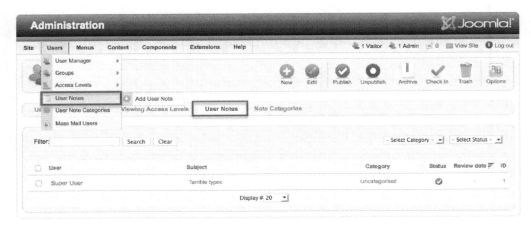

Figure 6: User Notes

Clean Up

Filtering for Categories in Article Manager

That is simply useful. Since Joomla 1.6 it was possible to filter categories in the article manager, but you did not see the articles of the subcategories. Now the filter logic include the articles of the subcategories too.

Linking New Menus with a Module

In Joomla 2.5 modules are NOT automatically created for each new menu type. This is not a bug, it's a feature :)
Not everyone used the core menu module, but used instead ones from a custom template or third party module. For that reason, menus did not automatically create a module in 1.6/1.7. This change confused people and created extra work. In Joomla 2.5, if there is no module associated with the menu, there is a link showing in the Menu Manager that you can click that will take you directly into a new module that you can create. You then have the choice of saving this standard menu module or cancelling out and using a different menu module.

Custom Text Filters are moved to the global configuration. They are filtering content for black and white listed tags based on your configuration and on role permission.

You can now choose to have **the administrator get a new message when a user creates an account**. This is useful when the New User Account Notification is set to Self. In that case the user receives an email after the registration with an activation link (*Figure 7*). After clicking that link the account is activated.

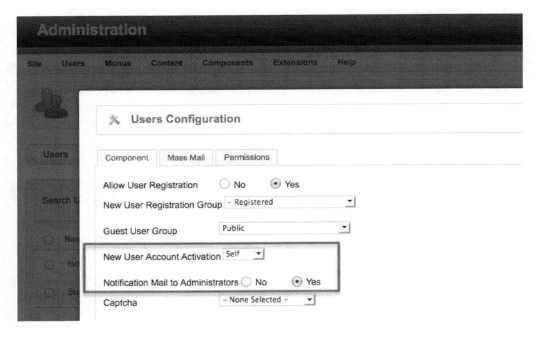

Figure 7: Administrator Notification

The extensive options in "Select a Menu Item Type" are not loaded unless you need them.

You will find a good summary in form of a presentation created by Mike Carson[35]

NEW FEATURES COMPARED TO JOOMLA 1.5

In comparison to **Joomla 1.5** the differences are huge and there is a long list of features and improvements.

- Here is a list of the most important changes in Joomla 1.6 and 1.7

- There will no longer be any sections. **Categories can be nested** as deeply as you would like

- The **access concept** is totally rebuilt.

The existing user groups used in Joomla 1.5 are still the same in Joomla 2.5 but they can be enhanced and renamed. Unlimited access levels can also be defined there. Users can be assigned to user groups and user groups can then be assigned to access levels.

- **Multiprocessing**

Copy and move operations, and the allocation of access levels can now be done in a batch process

---

[35] http://www.slideshare.net/carson3511/joomla-25-new-features-and-hidden-gems

- **Updates per mouse click**

A simple feature. The system detects available updates and initiates them after a click on the corresponding button.

- **Templates**

There have been many changes in the area of templates. There are now two administrator templates and three website templates.

- **Template styles**

Sometimes you may want to display a template with different options. You may want to create a page with a red background and another page with a blue one. Therefore, you will need template styles. Create as many versions (styles) of a template with different settings as you like and assign them to a menu link.

- **Template layouts**

Sometimes you may want to display only the output of a component or a module in a different layout without hacking the template. That's possible with template layouts.

- **Consistent user interface**

A successful example is the general save dialogue.
Save: content will be saved, you remain in editing mode
Save & Close: content will be saved, you leave the editing mode
Save & New: content will be saved; a new, empty editing mask appears
Save as copy: content will be saved as a copy, you remain in the editing mask

- **Minimum requirements**

The minimum requirements regarding your server environment and concerning your visitors' web browsers have increased.
Browser: Internet Explorer, version 7 or higher, Firefox, version 3 or higher, Safari, version 4 or higher
Server: PHP: minimum version PHP 5.2.4, MySQL: minimum version 5.04

- **Legacy Mode**

The legacy mode from Joomla 1.5 is no longer necessary. Legacy mode allowed the execution of components originally developed for Joomla 1.0, which have 'only' been adapted to Joomla 1.5. The procedure of adapting old components is offset by the development of 'native' Joomla 1.5 and 2.5 components, which use the Joomla Framework.

- **Search engine optimization**

    - You can now use unicode in URLs, which means you may now use special characters like 'ö' and 'ä' or Arabic or Hebrew characters in the URL.

    - You can allocate meta text and keywords to categories.

- You can combine the title of a site with the titles of its pages and decide on the order they will appear.
- **Modules** can be published time-controlled. The assignment options to menu items have been extended.
- **Multilingualism**

Joomla core now offers the possibility to create articles, categories and modules in several languages. With the new language switching plug-in and module you can filter the entire site for the selected language.

CodeMirror is the new editor, which is supplied in addition to TinyMCE. It is not a WYSIWYG editor but offers a convenient way to work with 'code-like' content, which will be displayed in a structured way with syntax highlighting.

- **Components**
    - The new redirect component enables redirections to URLs in order to avoid '404 not found' errors.
    - A new scalable search component has been introduced. It pre-searches the content, sorts results by relevance, suggests alternative search phrases, processes wide range of document types, etc.
    - The survey component has been eliminated.
- **New Release Cycle**

Every 18 months, a long term release of Joomla will appear.

- **Introduction of the Joomla platform**

Joomla consists of two parts

- the Joomla platform
- the Joomla content management system

There are many more very nice little features like the possibility to place a background image into a module or to display articles with page breaks in a tab or slider layout.

Chapter 6

Managing Content

A content management system is made for managing content - who would have thought?! So the next question is: What is content?

> In media production and publishing, content is information and experiences that may provide value for an end-user/audience in specific contexts (*Wikipedia* [36]).

Ok, I see, but what is it that provides value?

This question is indeed very hard to answer and quite individual but I think you now get the idea of content and a content management system like Joomla.

> A content management system is useful for managing information that provides value for your audience (*Hagen Graf :-)*).

TYPES OF CONTENT

In core Joomla you have *articles*, *categories*, *web links*, *banners*, *contacts* and *feeds*. I am not sure whether creating value with banners is possible but banners are also a kind of content. *Modules* can be used for content creation as well. Often you may want to enrich your content with files like photos and other media types. For this Joomla has its *Media manager*. This is what Joomla core provides as your toolbox to manage all these bits and pieces to create value to your audience. I am going to cover these tools in the next chapters.

If this isn't enough for you, you can enhance Joomla with so-called content construction kits[37] like K2[38], FlexiContent[39] or CCK jSeblod [40] and many other extensions, but that's another book entirely. :-)

---

[36] http://en.wikipedia.org/wiki/Content_%28media%29

[37] http://extensions.joomla.org/extensions/news-production/content-construction

[38] http://getk2.org

[39] http://www.flexicontent.org/

[40] http://www.seblod.com/

How to create an 'About Us' Page

To give you a first real challenge, let's create a first page on your new website. It will be an *about us* page on which you can write about your company, your project, or yourself. Most of the time, a page like this contains a title, text and perhaps a few images.

Static vs. Dynamic content

An "about us" page is usually created once, is accessible via a menu link, and in the future all you will have to do is change it as you go. It has a static character. A press release or blog entry, however, have a dynamic character.

- For static pages, in contrast to dynamic pages, the creation date and author do not really matter.
- Static pages are usually accessible via a menu link whereas dynamic pages can be accessed through lists.

The plan

The 'about us' page should consist of the following components:

- a title,
- a text,
- an image.
- The page should not appear on the front page.
- We want a link to the page in the top horizontal menu (top).

This may sound simple at first :-). Go ahead and log into the administration interface!

Step 1 - Create content

Go to the *Article Manager* (*Content* → *Article Manager*). There you might still see your unpublished sample data (*Figure 1*).

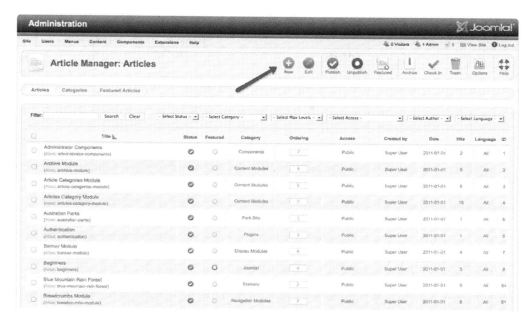

Figure 1: Article manager

Click the icon to get to the appropriate form and then add the title and text. In the upper pane, below the title, select "uncategorized" as a category. This category was created by installing the *example data*. The field *Featured* indicates whether the content should be displayed in the *featured blog layout*, which is mostly used as the front page. This still works in Joomla 2.5 but the terms can easily be misunderstood. Select *No*. In the editor window, you may now enter your text. Joomla comes with the default editor *TinyMCE* (*Figure 2*).

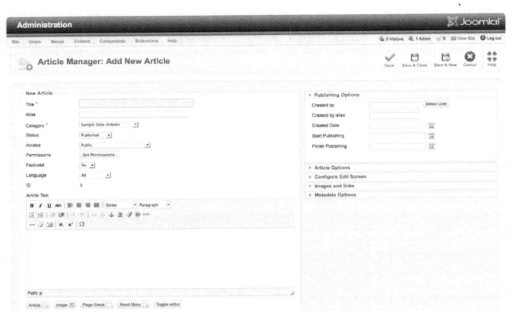

Figure 2: Article edit form

Inserting an image from a URL

As a first example we are going to use an already existing image on the web.
For example, this one: http://farm2.static.flickr.com/1198/898250237_78a0e75cba_m.jpg *(Figure 3)*

Figure 3: Example image

Move the cursor to the position in the text at which you would like to insert the image. Click on the image icon in the editor toolbar and paste the URL of the image to the pop-up window. Configure the image with a left alignment and use 10 pixels vertical and horizontal space (*Figure 4*).

Joomla! 2.5 - Beginner's Guide

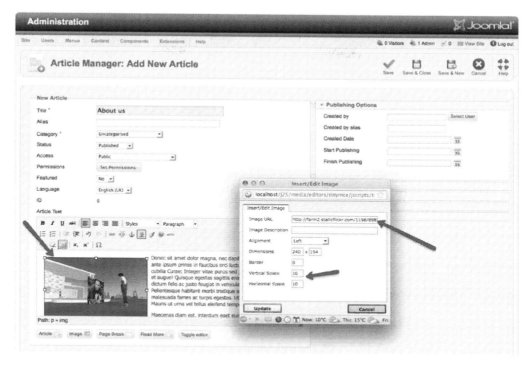

Figure 4: Insert image

The image will appear in your editor window. Click *Save* and your item is stored. There are several ways to save it:

- *Save* - Item is saved. Form is not closed. Used for saving when you still want to continue working.
- *Save & Close* - Item is saved and form will be closed.
- *Save & New* - Item is saved, form will be closed and a new empty article form is called.
- Exit the form.

Step 2 - Creating a Menu Link

The post has been created but is not appearing on the website. For it to appear, we need a link! Click the *New* icon in the *Menu manager* in the top menu (*Menu → Top*). Click the 'Select' button next to the field *Menu item type*. A window with various links will pop up. Click on the link *single article* (*Figure 5*).

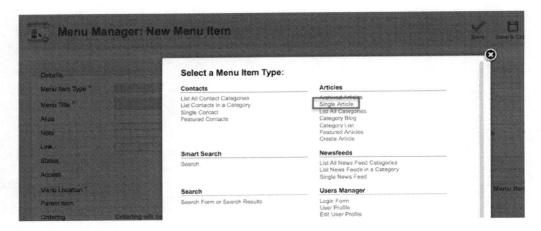

Figure 5: Assign an article to a menu item

Now you need to choose the desired article. Click the button *Select / Change* in the right pane (Select Article) to select it. You will see a search box with all articles. In case you can't find your article on the page right away, you can filter the list by typing a part of the article's title in the search box and then clicking on the title of the correct article in the result list (*Figure 6*).

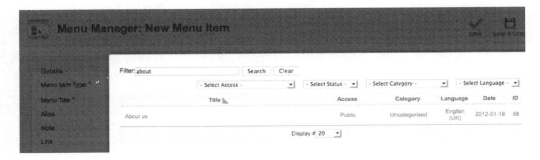

Figure 6: Menu type - single article - select article

Enter a title for the link "About us" and make sure that *top* is selected in the *menu location*. We can leave the remaining options with their settings for now.

Step 3 - 'About us' on the website

If you now load the frontend website, you will discover the new link in the top menu. Click it and you will see the *about us* content - congratulations on having created your first page (*Figure 7*).

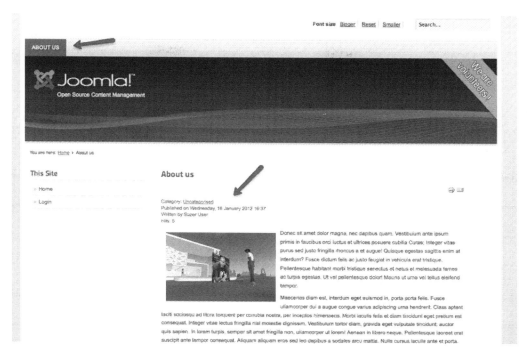

Figure 7: About us page

Step 4 - Image Upload

If your image is not already available on the Internet, you will need to upload it from your PC. Let's go through the example together. Go to the *Article Manager (Content → Article manager)*. If you can't find your article, locate it easily by using the search box. Select the article's title and the edit form will open. Delete the linked image from the text.

Below the editor window you will find the *Image* button. This button launches a dialog box to upload an image. You can choose between existing images or upload new ones (*Figure 8*).

Joomla! 2.5 - Beginner's Guide

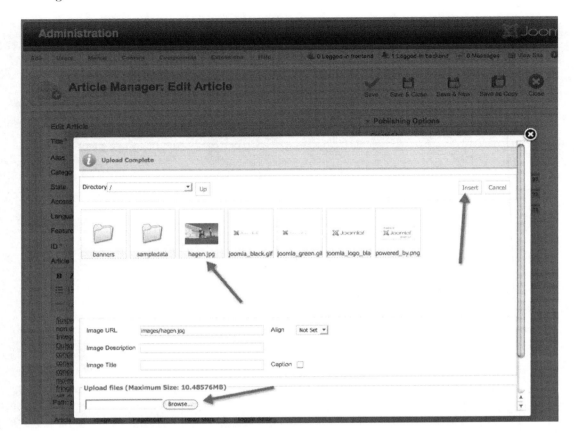

Figure 8: Image upload

Once the image has been inserted into the text, the formatting can be changed by using the *image icon* in the editor's toolbar. This separation of functions in Joomla was purposely chosen because you have the possibility to use different editors. The Joomla *Image* button will always remain the same but the image formatting in the editor might differ.

Attention: Joomla uses the images as they are. The images will not be resized!

To solve this issue, have a look at Brian Teemans blog entry: Making Joomla Idiot Proof[41] - May be FBoxBot[42] is available for Joomla 2.5 too when you read these lines.

---

[41] http://brian.teeman.net/tips-and-tricks/making-joomla-idiot-proof-part-1.html

[42] http://extensions.joomla.org/extensions/photos-a-images/articles-images/1162

A Typical Article

The following items usually have to be taken into consideration when it comes to creating an article on your website:

- a text with one or more images
- a teaser text for list views with a *read more* link pointing to the full article page
- the article should appear on the front page and needs no menu link
- nice to have: a scheduled publication date
- nice to have: a printer-friendly version for visitors who would like to print the article
- nice to have: an option to forward the article by email

Start

The article should appear on the front page of your website. If you deleted, did not install or change your sample data, your Joomla front page will look like the one in *Figure 1*. It is, of course, not a bad thing if posts should appear. :-)

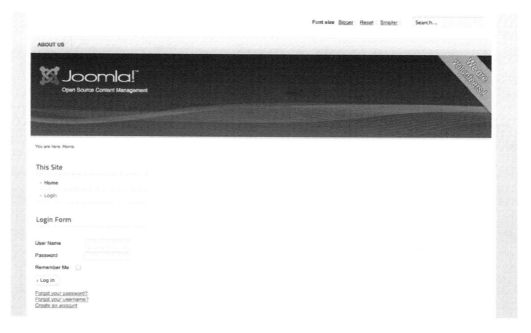

Figure 1: Empty website

When you log into the administration area, you will see an icon called *Add New Article*. You may either click on this icon or access the form via the main navigation *Content → Article Manager → Add New Article* (*Figure 2*)

Joomla! 2.5 - Beginner's Guide

Figure 2: Administration area

Article form

You are now in the article form, in which you will probably write all articles you will ever write in Joomla. A very important place! The form is structured as in *Figure 3*.

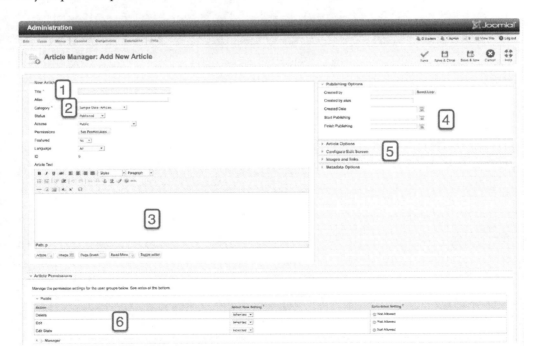

Figure 3: Entry form for contributions

The minimum requirement for an article is a title (1), a category (2), and a text (3). If you look at the form more closely, you will notice the help texts that appear when you move the mouse across the description of a field. I have marked the areas in the form in *Figure 3* with six digits.

Title

The most important part is the **title** or headline. The title appears as a headline on the website (usually in the biggest size of the HTML headline tags <h1>) and in the browser bar at the top *(you can enable or disable this behavior)*. The title is the foundation for the alias field below. The alias is automatically generated by Joomla when you save the article and the way it looks is configurable as well. Basically, the purpose of an alias is to have a simple, short and legible URL in the browser address bar, which can easily be used in e-mails or chats as well. In the example of http://example.com/first-article - *first-article* is the alias.

Category

This is about the classification or **categorization** of the article. Every article MUST be assigned to a **category**. If you explicitly do not want to categorize the article, you can assign the category *uncategorized*. This is especially useful for more static content pages like *legal notices* and the *About Us* page. In this area, other important attributes can be configured, including *State (published or not)*, who has Access *(Access, Permission depends on various settings)*, *Language* and *Featured*. *Featured* replaces the former attribute frontpage and ensures that the items are in a predefined blog layout for your website frontpage. The article *ID* is created after saving and consists of a serial number.

Text

In this section you can write your text, which should be of value to your audience . Sounds really easy, doesn't it?! :-)

Technically, you are dealing with a WYSIWYG editor *(What You See Is What You Get)* here. The editor converts your written text into HTML text format. Joomla uses the **TinyMCE**[43] editor as default configuration. TinyMCE is an independent open source project, which has so many functions that you could write a separate book about it. *(May not be a bad idea.)*

It basically works like any other word processor: write text, highlight text, then click on a toolbar icon and the function is applied or a dialog box opens.

The buttons below the input area are unusual and can be confusing at times. These buttons are Joomla specific and only have an indirect relationship with the editor. The Joomla core comes with five of these very practical additional buttons.

You can add more buttons by adding Joomla extensions:

1. **Article**: allows you to link to other existing Joomla articles

---

[43] http://tinymce.moxiecode.com/

2. **Image**: You can insert an existing image or photo from the *Media Manager* or upload a new image.

3. **Pagebreak**: inserts a pagebreak in your article

4. **Read More**: allows you to stipulate where to place the *read more* link

5. **Toggle Editor**: switches the editor on and off. If it is off, you will see the HTML code of your article.

Options

What was called *Parameter* in Joomla 1.5, is now called *Options* in Joomla 1.6, like, for example, the *Publishing Options*. Here you can specify who wrote the article (*Created by*). The user who created the article is usually allowed and responsible for making changes to the article later. Which name is really shown below the title at the webpage is configured in *Created by Alias*. The three fields below allow you to schedule the publishing. Simply enter the appropriate dates and Joomla takes care of the rest.

More Options

In this section you can configure many options by switching them on and off. You can change the article layout to suit the reader's and search engine's needs. Just start experimenting - it's the best way to learn.

Permission

The sixth and final area concerns the permissions for this article. This selection will help us in many places in Joomla 1.6 and I will cover this in chapter Users and Permissions.

SAMPLE ARTICLE

Let's create the article outlined above together:

A text with one or more images

Just write your text. To add an image or images, there are numerous possibilities:

1. The image is already available online, for example, on Flickr[44].

In this case, click the *image* icon in the editor toolbar and copy the image URL to the dialog box.

2. The image is already in the Joomla *Media Manager*.

In this case, click the *image* **button** below to select the image and insert it into your text (*Figure 4*).

---

[44] http://www.flickr.com/photos/hagengraf/5186325015/sizes/s/

Joomla! 2.5 - Beginner's Guide

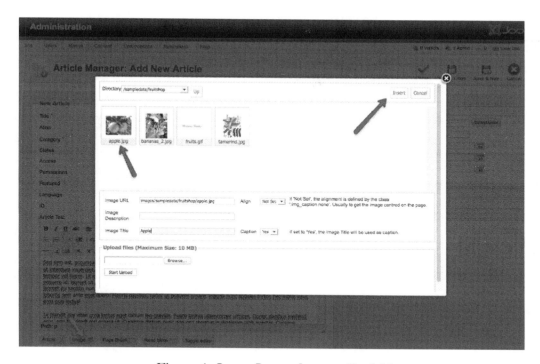

Figure 4: Insert Image from media field

3. The picture is on your hard disk.

This is the most complex case. Basically, you will also use the image button below the text. There you will find an upload dialogue through which you can upload your image "easily". Remember that Joomla will **NOT** resize the image. If you upload a photo from your digital camera, it will be displayed in its full original size (width > 3000 pixels). **You have to resize the image before uploading**.
If all goes well - congratulations!
If it doesn't work, this could be due to many things, such as lack of permissions in the directories of the media manager. At best, you will get an error message.

Once you have inserted the image from the media, you can select and format it by clicking the image icon in the editor's toolbar.

A teaser text for list views with a read more link to the full article

This is easy. Move the cursor to the position at which the *read more* link should appear and click on the *read more* button below the text area.

The article should appear on the frontpage and needs no menu link

Select *Yes* in the field *Featured* in Area 2.

A scheduled publication would be nice

Avoid this at first, so you don't have to wait for the article to appear on your website :-). If you would like to try it later with a different article, simply fill the fields *Start Publishing* and *Finish Publishing* with the appropriate information or select the dates by clicking the calendar icon.

A printer-friendly version of the article

If you do not know at this point where the global settings are located, have a look at the chapter Website and Content Configuration and verify the current settings. In area 5, you may switch the Show Printer icon to 'show'.

Forwarding of the article by e-mail

Simply set the options in area 5, switch the *Show Email Icon* to *show*.

RESULT

After saving you can reload your site and will see your article on the frontpage as in *Figure 5*.

Figure 5: Article on the frontpage

Media Manager

The media manager is Joomla's little Digital Asset Management System (DAM)[45]. If you are managing content, you will need a place to store the files. Files are all the images, PDFs and whatever you decide to mention in your content. Usually these digital assets consist of the file and additional meta data. In this case, we need an easy-to-use tool to manage our files. Let's have a look at what is possible with the Joomla core media manager.

How it works

To me it looks more like a file manager. Everyone knows the Windows explorer or the OSX finder. In Joomla they call it "media manager". It has a base directory where all the files are stored. You can look at your files in two different ways using your browser: via a *Thumbnail View* (*Figure 1*) and a *Detailed View* (*Figure 2*). It is possible to navigate through the folders by clicking on them.

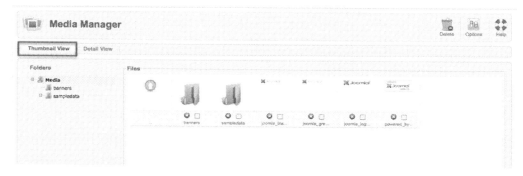

Figure 1: Media Manager - Thumbnail View

Figure 2: Media Manager - Detailed View

You can create as many additional folders as you wish. In the *Detailed View*, you are able to delete folders and files. You'll find the same structure in the Joomla administration backend as you can see in

---

[45] http://en.wikipedia.org/wiki/Digital_asset_management

your FTP client (*Figure 3*), but you have to be careful: In core Joomla you will also find a *media* directory. This directory is NOT the home of the media manager.

The home of the media manager in core Joomla is the *images* directory.

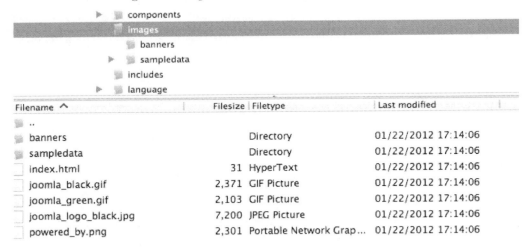

Figure 3: Media manager directory in ftp client

When you look in the toolbar you will discover the Options icon - go ahead and click on it (Figure 4).

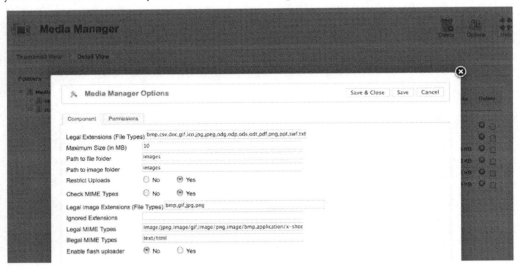

Figure 4: Media manager options

If you go through the options, you will notice that you can limit file types by extension, maximum size of a file and you can also separate *images* from *files*. Well, an image is a file, too, but I like the idea of separating them. The thumbnail view, e.g., makes a lot more sense for images but not for non-image files.

The biggest advantage of that separation is the possibility to *Restrict Uploads* to users lower than the manager role. You can allow registered users to upload images but you do not have to give permission to upload other files. This is, in some cases, very useful. The next options you see are MIME[46] types, nowadays often called *Internet Media Type*. If you are a Windows user, you usually only distinguish different file types by their extension. *Internet Media Type* is another way to recognize the type of a file even without a file extension. You can permit or forbid as many file types as desired.

The **Flash Uploader** is one of the most sophisticated features that is often forgotten about. In Joomla 1.5 it didn't always work properly but the version coming with Joomla 2.5 is excellent for uploading more than one file at a time. The *Flash Uploader* simply works and is easy to use! Try it! (*Figure 5*).

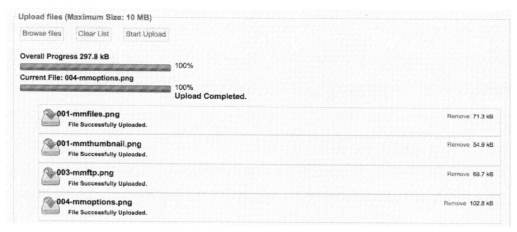

Figure 5: Media manager Flash Uploader

As you notice, the Joomla media manager is no rocket science[47] but it is a reliable, easy to use tool to manage your images and other files.

If you need a more sophisticated product, Joomla offers other solutions in the extension directory in the category File Management [48].

Media manager and the editor

Now you know about the central place of your files but how can you manage to connect them to your content?

---

[46] http://en.wikipedia.org/wiki/Mime_type

[47] http://www.urbandictionary.com/define.php?term=rocket+science

[48] http://extensions.joomla.org/extensions/core-enhancements/file-management

Anywhere you see an editor in Joomla, it is usually possible to add media from the media manager by clicking the image button below. We have already talked about this in Chapter A Typical Article (*Figure 6*).

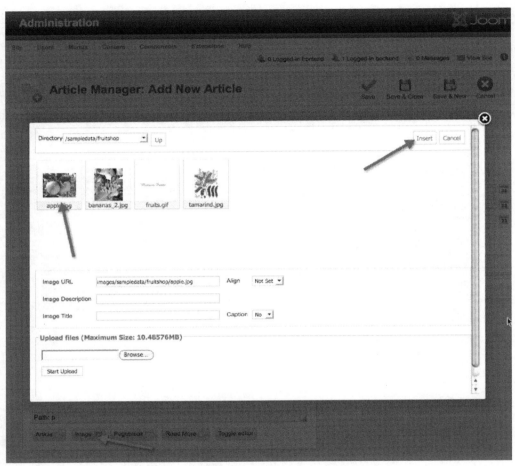

Figure 6: Media manager in content areas

Media Manager in other places

There are other places where the media manager plays a role, like in categories. It is possible to link an image to a category (*Figure 7*).

Figure 7: Media manager in category

This image will appear in a list of categories if you configure it in the *Menu Items Options*.

Contact Form

With a contact form the following question arises: "Is this content?". I think it is and have, therefore, written it as a sub chapter of the Managing Content chapter.

On a contact form it first becomes obvious that something like a CMS is being used. Manually created HTML pages cannot send emails as this requires a script language like PHP, for example, and a configured server. PHP scripts can be embedded as contact forms into HTML pages, but then that part of the website will often look different from the rest of the site. In Joomla the contact form is already integrated and you "only" have to configure it.

Ususally, if your Joomla is running on a web server at your provider, you won't have problems with sending emails. Locally, it's a bit more difficult because you would have to set up a mail server first. Generally, this is not a problem but it isn't really necessary. ;-)

Joomla sends emails in different ways. You will see an overview of this in *Global Configuration → Server* (*Figure 1*). Naturally, you would use the standard activated PHP Mail function (*read more: Website and Content Configuration*).

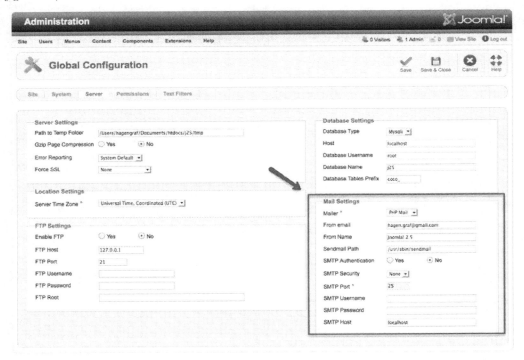

Figure 1: Mail Server Settings

Creating a contact

In order to include a contact on your site you need at least:

Joomla! 2.5 - Beginner's Guide

- a contact category
- a contact
- a link in a menu

Maybe you still have a category from the example data *(Sample-data contact)*. If not, go ahead and create one. In the next step you will create a new contact. To do so, open *Components* → *Contacts* in your administration area and click on the icon *New*. Then fill in the appearing form (*Figure 2*). I have labeled some areas in the screenshot for better orientation.

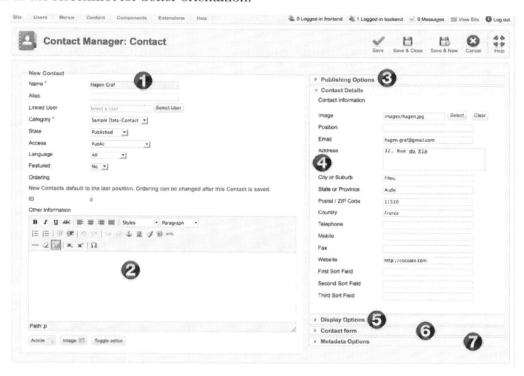

Figure 2: Create contact

1. The first and last name of the contact person, or the name of the department or company if it is not a person. The contact can be connected with an existing user account. He has to be assigned to a category, should be public *(State = Published)* and presumably not appear on the frontpage *(Featured = No)*.

2. The text area can be used for additonal information, e.g. opening hours or jurisdiction.

3. The *Publishing Options* relate to the user who can later make changes to that content, who created the content, and the timing for publishing. The latter is used rather seldomly for 'normal' websites.

4. In *Contact Details* there are numerous fields available, which you can choose to fill in or leave blank.

5. In *Display Options* you decide which fields will be displayed. This area is important as you specify here whether a contact form will be shown or not (*Show Contact Form*). You can also specify whether the sender should receive an email copy and you'll be able to configure some spam protection settings (*Banned E-Mail, Banned Subject*, etc). Against "real" spammers, however, this protection is rather "pathetic".

6. In the field *Contact Redirect*, you can enter another email adress to which the contents of the form should be sent.

7. The Metadata Options are, like the Publishing Options, available on each single page (Read more: Why SEO is important for you).

Creating a menu item

You now have a contact but still no form on your website. That is exactly what we are going to create in this next step. Due to the fact that you can link nestable categories to contacts, you may either have a single contact form or many of them. It is definitely possible to create a contact form for each employee of a big company like Volkswagen (approx. 370,000 employees). How does such a dynamic CMS display this on a website?

To manage this, Joomla has its own *Menu Manager* with different layouts. In the *Menu Manager*, you get to decide whether you want to have a list of contacts or categories or just a single contact form. At first glance this may seem somewhat confusing but it is well thought out and helpful.

Let's link a single form in the menu for the contact we have just created. Open *Menus - Top* and click the *New* icon. You need three things for a menu link:

1. the *Menu Item Type* (type of link) for displaying the site and, depending on your choice, a contact or a category

2. a text displayed as a link

3. the menu, in which the link should appear

For number 1, click on the *Select* button next to the field *Menu Item Type*. A window will open and you will see a choice of types. Click *Single Contact* (*Figure 3*).

Joomla! 2.5 - Beginner's Guide

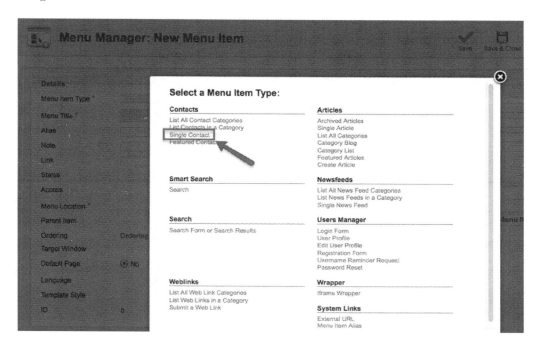

Figure 3: Choice of menu types

The window will close again. Since you only want one contact, you will now have to choose the contact in *Required Settings* (*Figure 4*).

Figure 4: Choose contact

At last, insert the text for the link (*Menu Title*) and then save everything. The menu is already registered correctly by opening the form. On your website, an additonal link in the *Top Menu* should be appearing, which is linked to the corresponding contact (*Figure 5*). You can get to the actual contact form by clicking the plus sign in the right field. Now you can send messages via your website.

Figure 5: Contact at website

Figure 6: Contact form

Chapter 8
Statuses, Trash and Check-Ins

In Joomla your content can have several statuses. Depending on the type of content there can be a minimum of three statuses: **published**, **unpublished** and **trash**. What does that mean? After saving your fresh content for the first time, it exists in the Joomla database and depending on its status, it will appear (or not) in different areas of your website.

The usual life cycle of content in Joomla is:
1. unpublished until you are finished with editing and reviewing
2. *published* or *scheduled* (and possibly *featured* on the frontpage)
3. still *published* but may be removed from the frontpage
4. archived

Sometimes it is necessary to *unpublish* content and sometimes you may put it into the *trash*. The content itself will, of course, continue to exist. It has not been deleted. You can filter most of the tables in the administration interface by the desired statuses and assign different statuses to your content as often as you would like.

Unpublished
No website visitor is able to see the content. It is the phase in which you edit and review your content.

Published
It depends on the users' and visitors' permissions whether they will be able to view the content but generally the content on your website should be visible because it has been published!

Featured
The *featured* 'feature' is a switch you can use for your most important and latest content and is usually shown at the frontpage. It is an additional status because it is only relevant to articles. This is why it is possible for an article to be *unpublished* and *featured*.

Archived
There will come a time when you'll start thinking about an archive for your articles. Just set the status to *archived* and you've almost created an archive. Joomla knows the creation date of your articles and offers an archive module to be shown on your site. The archive module is included in the example data.

If it is not available, just create one in *Modules* → *New* →*Archived Articles*. Your articles will then be shown like in *Figure 1*. Read more in chapter Modules.

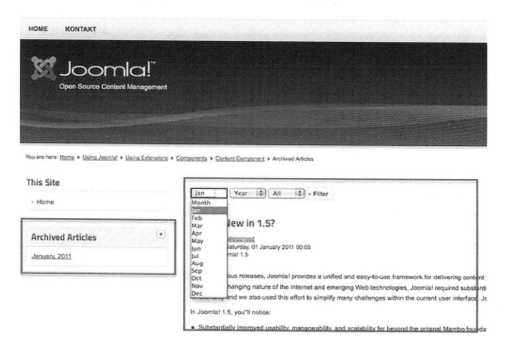

Figure 1: Joomla Archive

Trash

The second last status is *trash*. If a content item ends up here it still exists and can be retrieved. You can place modules, menu items, categories, articles, contacts, and even more content in your trash. You can see the contents of your trash can by filtering it (*Figure 2*).

Figure 2: Trash

In the filtered view the *Trash* icon changes to *Empty trash*. This is your opportunity to delete content.

Check In

The *Check In* icon in Joomla may not be the kind you know from Foursquare[49] or other location-based services. It is a security feature for editing your content. As soon as a user starts editing content, Joomla locks this content for all other users. The advantage of this behavior is that changes by another user cannot be overwritten. That's a very convient feature. One big problem, however, appears when the user editing the content accidentally closes the browser window, allows the session to expire or the power plant shuts off the power or ... you get my point :-).
Then the content is locked and no one else can edit it!

No one else (except a user with proper permission, e.g. you as the administrator) can *check in* the content again to allow others to edit it. Unfortunately, you will only notice unchecked content by a small lock being displayed near the title (*Figure 2*) or by a cry for help from one of your users :-).

---

[49] http://en.wikipedia.org/wiki/Foursquare_%28social_network%29

Joomla! 2.5 - Beginner's Guide

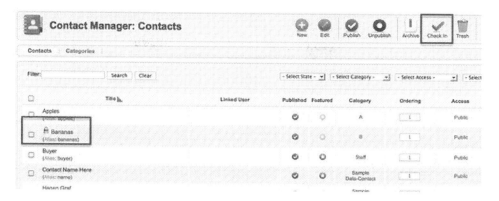

Figure 3: Check In

Chapter 7

Structure Your Content with Categories

Joomla articles must be categorized. Generally spoken, categorization is the process of recognizing, differentiating and understanding something through abs creating as many categories traction. This may sound rather complicated but proves very useful when managing several articles.

Joomla offers the possibility of creating as many categories as you wish. It is possible to build nested categories and an article has to be related to one of these categories.

Newspapers, for example, use categories to better differentiate between their articles. Here is an example from a Joomla template[50] (*Figure 1*).

Figure 1: Gavick Template December 2009

---

[50] http://demo.gavick.com/joomla15/dec2009/

They are using the category *World News* and under this category there are additional categories like *Politics*, *World*, *War*, *Disasters* and *more*. Sometimes two levels are sufficient like in this example; sometimes you may need more. In Joomla 1.5 it was not possible to have more than two levels. With Joomla 2.5 you can have as many levels as you want. Joomla no longer has sections - only categories.

In the *Category Manager* (*Administration* → *Content* → *Category Manager*), you can manage your category tree and filter up to 10 levels (*Figure 2*).

Figure 2: Category Manager

Like an article, a category consists of a title, a description and many other attributes and options. It can have an additonal image that can be used in different layouts. The image can be selected in the basic settings. A category can also contain images in the description (*Figure 3*).

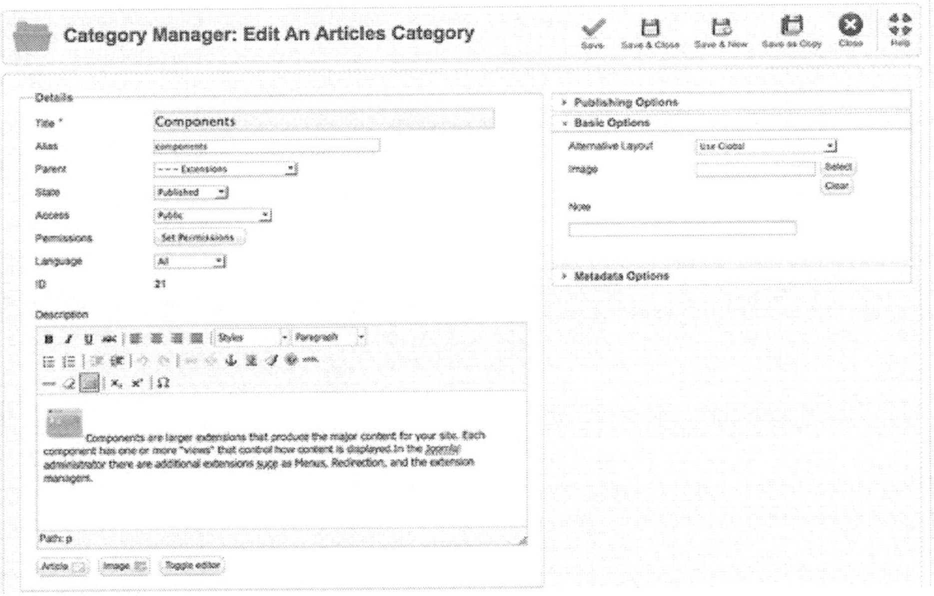

Figure 3: Category Edit Form

When you access your Joomla website you can see exactly these categories in the example data. The navigation uses links to the categories to show all the articles and sub categories (*Figure 4*). Even the breadcrumb navigation reflects this structure.

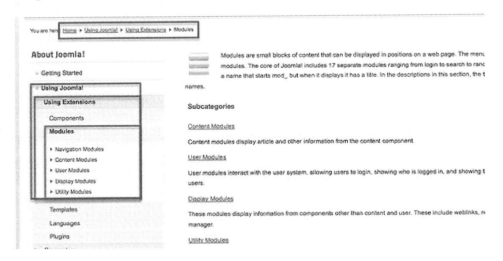

Figure 4: Categories as menu links on the website

In the *Menu Manager* (*Administration* → *Menu* → *About Joomla*), you can see these menu items, which link to the articles in a category (*Figure 5*).

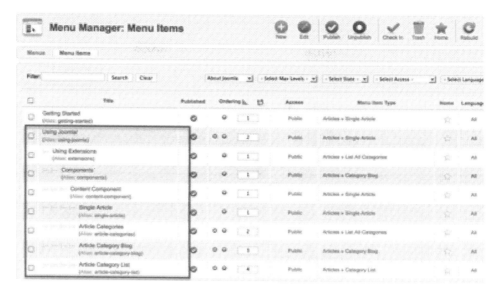

Figure 5: Categories as menu links on the website

You can choose from different layouts for the articles. In *Figure 5* you can see which layout is used for which link. You can select the layout in the edit form of a menu item (*Figure 6*).

Possible layouts:

- a list of all categories
- a blog layout (like on the frontpage)
- a category list

Depending on the layout you have plenty of options to configure the appearance and behavior of sub categories and articles.

Figure 6: Category layouts

A list of all categories

This layout lists all the sub categories from one chosen category *(Figure 7)*.

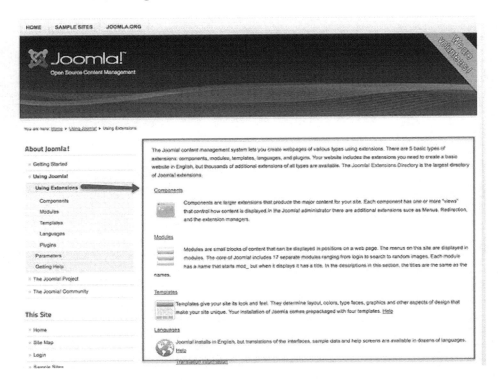

Figure 7: Layout All Categories

In this case the category description from the top level category *Extensions* is shown. One level of sub categories with their descriptions is also shown on the page, even empty categories. The articles in the top level category are hidden. Example: *Administration* → *Menus* → *About Joomla* → *Using Extensions* → *Edit*.

A blog layout (like on the frontpage)

The blog layout lists all the articles from one chosen category *(Figure 8)*.

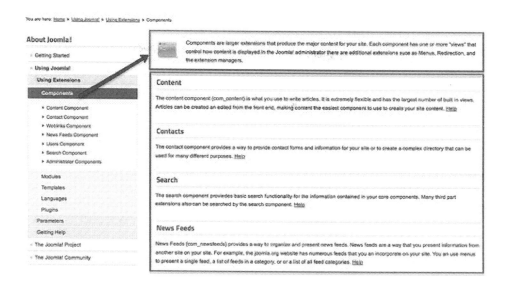

Figure 8: Layout Blog

In this case the category description from the category *Components* is shown. All the articles related to *Components* are shown with their teaser text in one column. More columns are also possible. The first seven articles in the top level category are hidden. Example: *Administration* → *Menus* → *Components* → *Edit* (*Figure 9*).

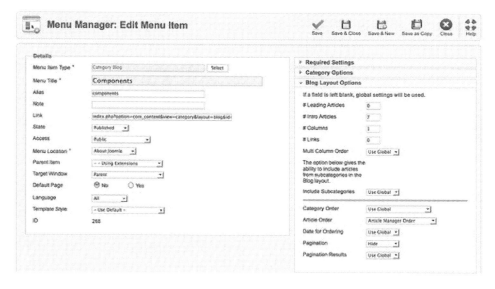

Figure 9: Layout Blog settings

A category list

The category list layout lists all the articles from one chosen category in a table structure *(Figure 10)*.

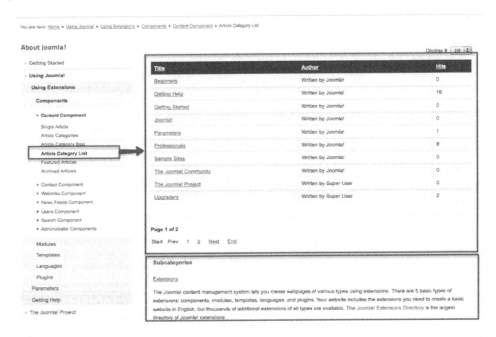

Figure 10: Layout Category List

In this case the category description from the category named *Joomla* is shown. All the articles related to *Joomla* are shown in a configurable table. You can choose to have parts of the table hidden and various sorting options are available. Example: *Administration → Menus → Components → Article Category list → Edit.*

Conclusion

The category system in Joomla 2.5 is very powerful and easy to use. You can easily structure your entire website by using a set of nested categories in a very user-friendly way. One article can be assigned to one category.

Chapter 9
Website and Content Configuration

Joomla has different levels of configurating options. These options are transmitted from the highest to the lowest level.

- Global configuration
- Options for articles, components, modules, plug-ins, languages and templates

GLOBAL CONFIGURATION

In the *Global Configuration* section you can define all the settings that are valid for the entire website. Most values of the variables are saved in the *configuration.php* file. Vital information like user name, database name and password for the database server, for instance, and 'lesser' parameters such as the pre-determined length of displayed lists are stored in this file. The work area is divided into five tabs:

- Site Settings
- System Settings
- Server Settings
- Permissions
- Text Filter Settings

The work area of every tab consists of dozens of fields, check boxes, switches and text areas. The easiest way to get a glimpse is to move your mouse across the labels to read the help text, which appears in a small yellow tooltip (*Figure 1*).

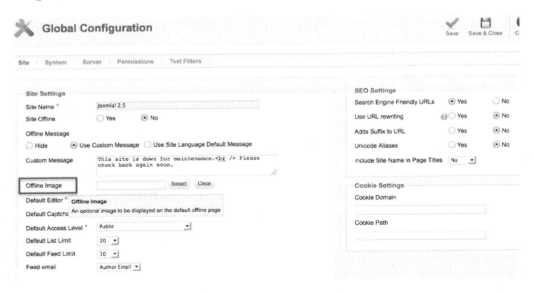

Figure 1: Tooltips

Most of the options are self-explanatory. I'll mention a few settings that are new in Joomla 1.6 with greater detail.

Site Settings

The *Site settings* have a new field for setting the default access level for new users. Configurable access levels are a new feature (*Read more: Users and Permissions*).

The *Metadata settings* now contain the option to add *Content Right* data. Joomla will add your data to the meta declaration *rights* in your HTML code. Depending on your search engine optimization (SEO) 'religion', it is good or bad to have this declaration in your meta profile. Now Joomla serves both :-)

```
<meta name="rights" content="© 2011 cocoate.com EURL, France" />
```

Figure 2: Site settings

In *SEO settings*, the new options are

- *Unicode Aliases*

  You set aliases for article titles. With this feature, URLs like http://example.com/所有一起 are possible.

- *Include Site Name in Page Titles*

  With this feature the article title will appear in the browser's document title bar.

Cookie settings are a wonderful feature for evaluating a cookie on different sub domains. You will need this feature if you have a site (*example.com*) and one or more sub domains (*blog.example.com*) and you want to offer your users the service to login on *example.com* and post on *blog.example.com*. Without this feature, the user should login again to post something on *blog.example.com*.

System Settings

The user and media settings are no longer in this area. You will now find them in the *User* and *Media Manager*.

The cache settings are different because the underlying cache system was rewritten and now provides more possibilities. In general, a cache makes your sites faster by storing parts of the HTML in files. The web server can deliver these files extremly fast. It is possible to cache pages, component views and modules. You can purge and clear the cache in *Site → Maintenance*.

Server Settings

All the server settings are the same as in Joomla 1.5. Nevertheless, I'll mention the option *Force SSL*. This option is getting more and more attention. You can offer your users a completely secured traffic. It is necessary to have SSL configured in your web server and you need a SSL certificate.

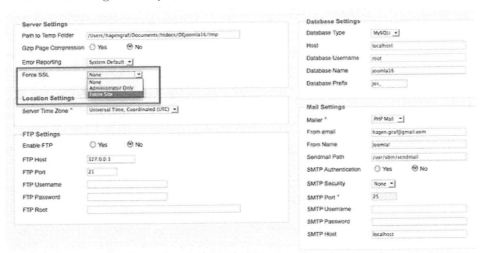

Figure 3: Server settings - SSL

Permissions

Here is the place to set your global permissions for your user groups. Fortunately, it is not always necessary to change the default settings. If you change the setting for a group, it will apply to this and all sub groups, components and content. Basically you allow, deny and inherit the permissions *Site Login*, *Admin Login*, *Offline Access*, *Super Admin*, *Access Component*, *Create*, *Delete*, *Edit*, *Edit State* and *Edit Own*. Every group has their own set of permissions (*Figure 4*).

Figure 4: Global group permissions

Text Filters

The text filters are a concept, which allows you to search contributed text for patterns like HTML tags and filter them (*Figure 5*). It's possible to set different filters for different groups. Let's say a registered user is allowed to post text with HTML tags inside but without an iframe. Only your individual group 'iframers' has the right to post iframes! These filters are active for content of the whole website.

Joomla! 2.5 - Beginner's Guide

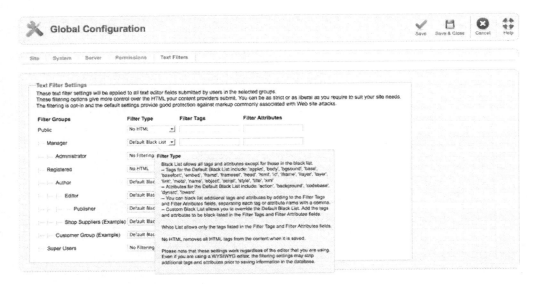

Figure 5: Article options - Text Filter

Chapter 10
Templates

The template is one of the most important pieces of a website. It provides the appearance, the design. It motivates new visitors to stay on your site and explore. Regular visitors and users appreciate being on a site with a beautiful and useful design. Think of other products, for instance. A car needs a good engine and tires but one of the most important reasons for buying one is often the design. Even if the design is not the main reason, it is often a trigger to contemplate the idea of purchasing and may cause a buyer to consider more tangible reasons. If the design is well-made, people expect the rest to be well-made, too. (*Figure 1, Figure 2*)!

Figure 1: Car with stickers (Richardmasoner CC BY-SA 2.0[51])

---

[51] http://www.flickr.com/photos/bike/201402884

Figure 2: Red car (FotoSleuth CC BY-SA 2.0[52])

Both of these cars are made for different target groups. They are an example of different approaches in design.

Web design is somewhat like a handcraft. Possessing skills in techniques like HTML, CSS, JavaScript, PHP, image editing and many others is imperative. Joomla is only one more tool in your toolbox.

A good template is not only about colors and graphics. The shape and positioning of the content is just as important. The website has to be user-friendly and reliable. Exactly this challenge reminds me of the two cars again.

Web design is still a young profession. A web designer often has to deal with low bandwith, incompatible browsers, inexperienced content editors and other people involved in the process of creating a 'good' website. The creation of a Joomla website is often a process, in which everyone involved learns a lot. Good web design is hard work. :-)

JOOMLA AND TEMPLATES

Joomla is known for its quality and simplicity. In Joomla a single page is generated by the HTML output of one *component*, several *modules* and the template. Each page is accessible via a unique URL. Take the front page as an example. The content component produces the HTML output for the articles in the middle (*Figure 3*). The blocks next to the articles are different *modules*. You can combine the HTML output from **one** *component* with the HTML output of **any number of** *modules*. Existing *modules* can also be reused on other pages.

---

[52] http://www.flickr.com/photos/51811543@N08/4978639642

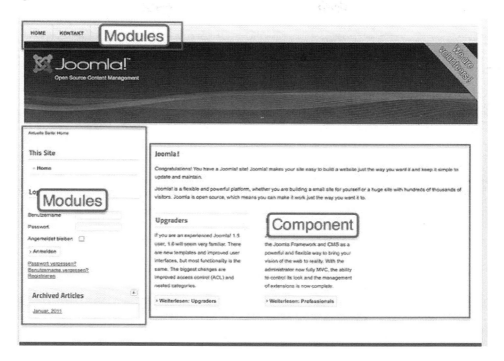

Figure 3: Joomla front page

POSITIONS

You must know, of course, at which point you can assign modules at all. For this purpose, each template provides so-called *positions*. In order to see these *positions* you have to enable the *Preview Module Positions* switch (*Extension - Template Manager - Options*). After that, you can access your website by using the parameter *tp=1* (http://localhost/index.php?tp=1). You'll see the emphasized module positions and their names (*Figure 4*). In *Extensions - Module Manager* you can assign one of these positions to a module. If you need the module at different positions, you may also copy it. Since Joomla 2.5 there is an easier way added to the backend. You will see them by clicking on the icon that has now changed, next to the name of the template in (Extension - Templates Manager) (*Figure 5*)

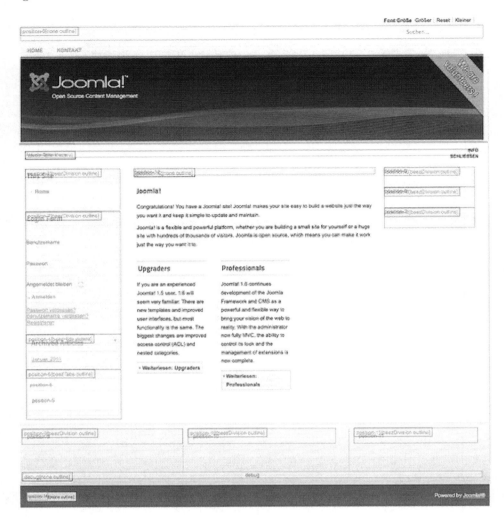

Figure 4: Module positions

Figure 5: Preview Icons

CORE TEMPLATES

Joomla core comes with three site templates and two administrator templates. You can see a preview in *Extensions* → *Template Manager* → *Tab Templates* (*Figure 6*).

Figure 6: Site templates

The Atomic template is an example of what a basic template looks like. In the chapter Create a New Template Using Atomic, we will use this template as a base to create our own template. The *Beez5* template is the HTML 5 Version of *Beez2*. Also for the Administration, another template is available. *(Figure 7)*

Figure 7: Admin templates

STYLES

Styles are a new feature since Joomla 1.6. They offer the possibility to create and use different versions of one template. A template has a minimum of one style. In this style, configurations can be made depending on the template, such as changing the colors or uploading the header logo. You may set the default style for your site in *Extensions → Template Manager → Styles*. You can filter between *Site* and *Administrator Styles* by choosing the location filter. The default template Beez2 comes with two predefined styles: *default* and *Parks Site*.

You can create additional styles by copying them. Each style can be assigned to a menu item. If you would like a green background on your site when people click on *menu item A*, for example, and a blue background when they click on *menu item B*, you can assign the corresponding styles (*Figure 8*).

Figure 8: Assign a style to a menu item

You will find more on templates in the chapter Working with Templates.

Chapter 11
Navigation

Photo: http://www.flickr.com/photos/62904109@N00/5214296452 CC BY 2.0

Every site needs an easy to understand navigation, otherwise it will not be possible for a user to find what he is looking for. This may sound simple but is not easily done. In a perfect world it should be possible to access any page on a website with two or three clicks. Another fact is, that often, if not always, your visitors will come from a search engine or social media site and will land anywhere on your site but your frontpage. This is a reason to think about a "Home" button on every page!

A website often has a primary and a secondary navigation. The primary navigation is usually at the top or on the left or right side. Secondary navigation is at the bottom or at the top, but mostly a bit smaller than the primary navigation. It contains links like contact, about us and legal notices. The idea behind this is to have these links at the site but not at a very important position.

As a general rule, do not put more than four to eight links in a navigation level.

Breadcrumbs

A 'breadcrumb trail' is a navigation aid. The term comes from the trail of breadcrumbs left by Hansel and Gretel[53] in the Brothers Grimm fairytale. Usually breadcrumbs are positioned horizontally on the top of a web page. Two structures are used:

- showing links back to each previous page the user clicked through to get to the current page
- showing the parent pages of the current one

Breadcrumbs are a way to prevent visitors from feeling lost on your site. Ideally visitors should always know where they are on the site and how to go back. Joomla provides a breadcrumb module for this task and most templates have a breadcrumb position reserved for it (*Figure 1*).

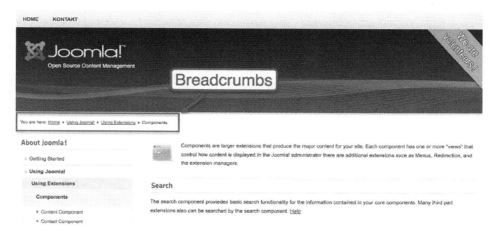

Figure 1: Breadcrumbs

Joomla Menus

Joomla navigations are created by so-called menus. You can create as many menus as you need for your website. Each menu may contain any number of nested menu items and you can even filter the level. A menu item is assigned to a component or an external URL. Modules and template styles can be assigned to menu items. In the example data, a few menus are shown that have already been created.

Let's have a look at two examples of primary navigation with static pages and dynamic categories.

---

[53] http://en.wikipedia.org/wiki/Hansel_and_Gretel

First example: a static catalog or book structure

Sometimes you need a navigation for a book, a catalog or a guide. You'll find this configuration in the example data in the *About Joomla* menu. Let's say we're writing a short book consisting of three chapters. The navigation should be linked to all pages and look like *figure 2*.

Figure 2: Static book structure

Preparation

Create a book structure with a few chapters.

- The Joomla book
    - Introduction
    - Content
        - How to use A
        - How to use B
    - Templates

Before creating menu items, you have to create individual articles (pages) first. Go to *Content → Article Manager → Add new article* (*Figure 3*). You may assign the *uncategorized* category to these articles or you can create a *book* category in advance and assign it to the chapters.

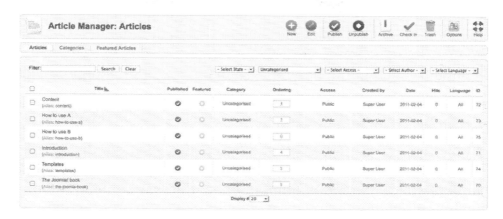

Figure 3: Six 'book chapters'

Step 1: Creating the menu

You can use an already existing menu as your *primary links* or you can create a new one by accessing *Menus* → *Menu Manager* → *Add new Menu* and filling out the form (*Figure 4*).

Figure 4: Add new menu

Step 2: Creating the menu items

Go to *Menus* → *Primary links* and add the six articles as links. Choose *Single Article* as *Menu Item Type*. Select the article and enter a *Menu Title* (*Figure 5*). If you have forgotten how to do that, have a look at the chapter How to create an 'About Us' Page.

Figure 5: Primary menu items

Step 3: Creating and assigning the module

This step is a bit tricky. You now have the articles, the menu and the menu items but you'll also need a module to position on your site. Let's go ahead and create one. Go to *Extensions* → *Modules* → *New Module* and fill in the form. In the Field *Select Menu* in *Basic Settings*, choose *Primary links*. Select *Yes* in the field *Show Sub menu items* (*Figure 6*).

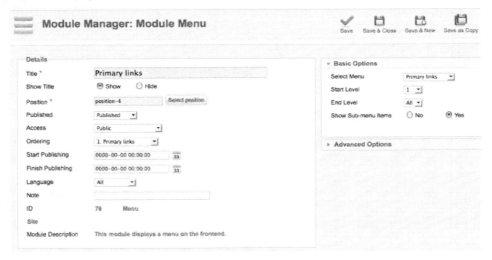

Figure 6: Primary links module

The last step is the template position. Click the *Select position* button, filter for template *Beez_20* and choose *position-4*. Save everything and you're done.

Figure 7: Select template position

SECOND EXAMPLE: LINKING TO CATEGORIES (NEWS MAGAZINE)

It is possible to link to a few pages like in the first example but what will you do if you have thousands of articles? The answer is easy in Joomla:
Build a structure with categories, assign the articles and link it to a category layout.

Preparations

We'll need a few categories with articles:

Categories:

- News
  - World
  - Africa
  - Europe
- Technology
  - Internet
  - Cars

Create them or use existing categories (Read more: Structure Your Content with Categories).

Step 1: The menu

It's up to you how to continue. The easiest way is to use the existing Primary Links menu. But if you want, you can create a News Menu, like me.

Step 2: The menu items

When dealing with categories you have to think about what should be shown after you have clicked on the link. The expected behavior in our case is
- Category News = all news should come up

- Category News → World = we want world news only

    and so on (*Figure 8*).

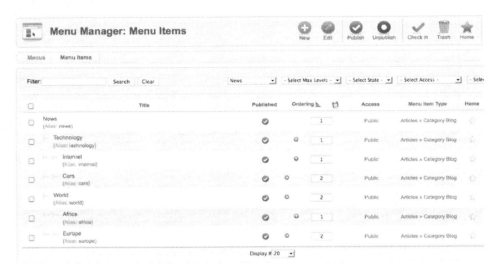

Figure 8: Menu items in News menu

To achieve the expected behavior, create a menu item with the type *Category Blog*. In *Required settings*, choose your newly created category *News*. In *Blog Layout Options*, choose *Include Sub Categories - All* and *# Leading Articles = 0*. Continue with creating nested menu items for each additional category and you're done (*Figure 9*).

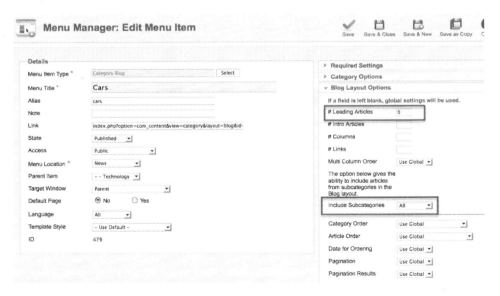

Figure 9: Category Options

Now you can handle thousands of articles. Your navigation is prepared for that and your visitors will understand the system immediately (*Figure 10*).

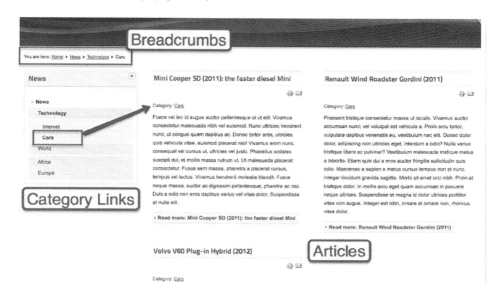

Figure 10: Articles in category structure

Some tweaking

As you have seen, there are nearly infinite possibilities of setting options. Many things are possible and there is usually a way to achieve your goals. Concerning the navigation design, it is possible to filter the level of the menu items in the module. It is possible, for example, to put

- the first level of our *News* menu at the top position and the second and third level in the the left or right sidebar
- the whole menu on top and use drop down menus (depending on the capabilities of the template)

If you play around a bit, you will find a solution for nearly every case. The Joomla navigation system may be a bit complex on one hand but is very powerful on the other.

Joomla! 2.5 - Beginner's Guide

Chapter 12

Users and Permissions

People simply try to use the Joomla website that you have created for them - in an active or passive way. The better the experience, the better the website will be perceived. Joomla - as every CMS differentiates between visitors and registered users with different permissions. Visitors usually arrive via search engines or social media site recommandations and can become users by registrating. Already registered users mostly know what they are looking for and come to your site with certain expectations.

The more users your site has, the more complex the topic users and permissions becomes. In versions preceding Joomla 1.6, there was a static system consisting of user groups, permissions and access levels that could not be changed. With Joomla 2.5, the old system is still alive as the default configuration of a very powerful so-called access control list (ACL)[54].

Every site access will be evaluated by a *Permission Group*, even an access from a visitor. After registering on your Joomla website, the user will automatically become a member of a *Permission Group*. The group has predefined permissions and belongs to an *access level*. One *Access Level* can have any number of *Permission Groups*. One group can have any number of users/visitors. Permissions can be passed down and overwritten in several places.

Let's begin by having a look at the registration process.

REGISTRATION AND LOGIN

The first registration process in your website's life cycle was completed with the installation of Joomla. In the last step you were prompted for a user name, an email address and a password. The person who installed Joomla is now the super duper administrator, who has permission to do everything on the site. This is why every Joomla website has at least one user account. It's up to this user only to modify the behavior of the site in *Users - User Manager - Options (Figure 1)*.

---

[54] http://en.wikipedia.org/wiki/Access_control_list

Figure 1: User options

On your Joomla site, you can create as many users as you would like. You can also allow visitors to register themselves. Depending on the their permissions, users can create their own content and/or view content that has been created for them in particular.

User options

The form has three tabs

- **Component**

  In this area you are able to configure whether a registration is possible or not. One of the new features since Joomla 1.6 is the possibility to configure in which user group the guests are in and in which user group the registered users are in by default.

- **Mass mail**

  It is possible to send a mass mail to your users. In this tab you can configure the static email settings.

- **Permissions**

  In this tab you can manage the permission settings for every user group.

Log in

Visitors can register on the website. Joomla, therefore, offers a login module, which can be positioned at the site (*Figure 2*).

Figure 2: Login module

This module can be configured with many additonal features like customized text, SSL encryption and login / logout redirection. Have a closer look at *Extensions - Module Manager* (*Figure 3*).

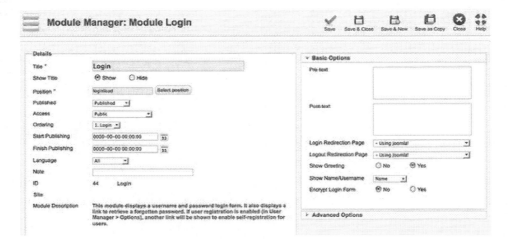

Figure 3: Login module options

The advantage of the form, which is delivered by login module, is that there is no necessity for the user to click a link before the log in form appears. If this behavior is not necessary or you don't want to have the login form as a module, it is also possible to create the form via a component. Therefore you have to create menu items with the appropriate menu item types concerning your needs (*Figure 4*).

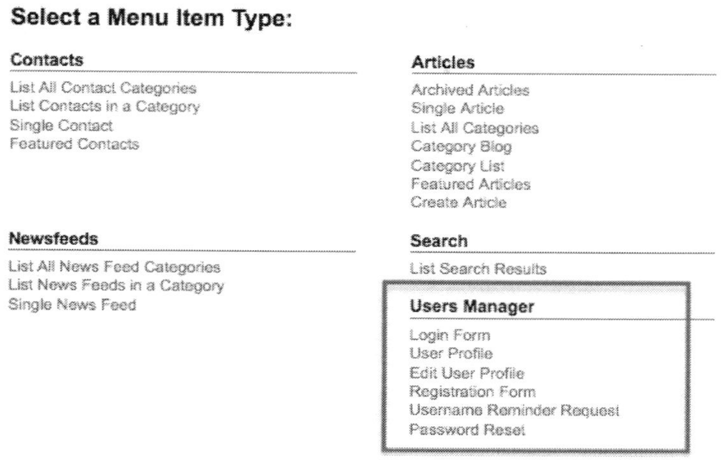

Select a Menu Item Type:

Contacts
List All Contact Categories
List Contacts in a Category
Single Contact
Featured Contacts

Articles
Archived Articles
Single Article
List All Categories
Category Blog
Category List
Featured Articles
Create Article

Newsfeeds
List All News Feed Categories
List News Feeds in a Category
Single News Feed

Search
List Search Results

Users Manager
Login Form
User Profile
Edit User Profile
Registration Form
Username Reminder Request
Password Reset

Figure 4: Menu item types for users

Additional profile fields

In the past it was only possible with additional extensions, to have additional fields in the registration form. To solve that issue and to connect the user data to the contact component, Joomla 2.5 core comes with a plug-in called *User Profiles*. In *Extensions - Plug-in Manager* you can activate and configure the plug-in (*See also Contact component*) The module provides several additional fields, even a *Terms of service* option, which user have to check during the registration process to accept the terms of service (*Figure 5*).

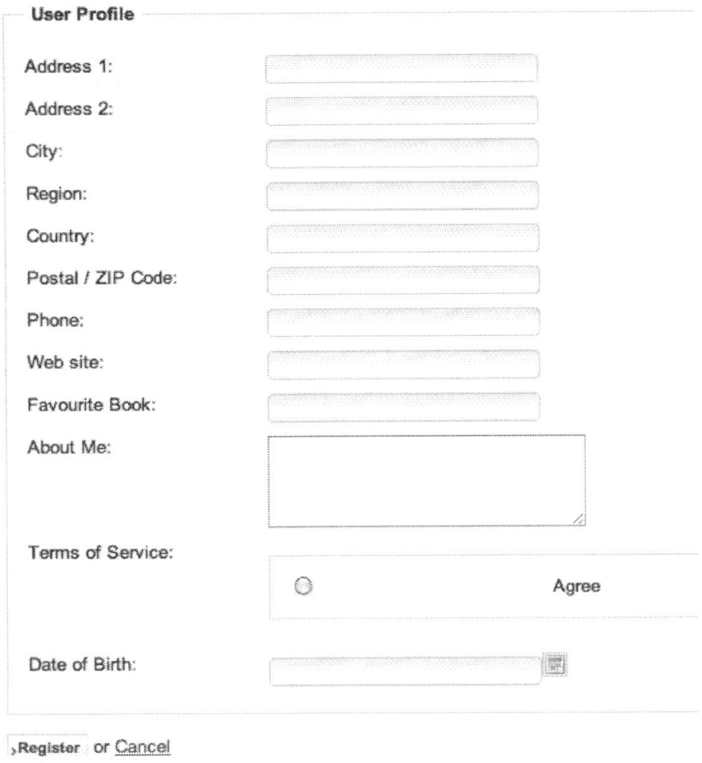

Figure 5: Additional profile fields

Tip: For better membership management functionality including extended registration form, additional profile and registration fields, membership approval workflows, profile tabs, etc. a membership management extension like e.g. Community Builder[55] is needed.

USER GROUPS

The idea of a user group is to create sets of permissions.

"If you want to be an author on our site, you'll need the following permissions."

Instead of assigning these permissions to every user they are assigned to a group. The user can be assigned to one or more groups. Imagine you have 10.000 users in four different groups. It's easy for the administrator to manage the permissions for the groups. Without groups you have to change every user account manually. If you use groups you only have to change permissions once!

In Joomla 2.5 it's up to you to configure any number of user groups. In *User Manager - Groups*, you have an overview of all the groups, which are in core Joomla (*Figure 6*).

---

[55] http://extensions.joomla.org/extensions/clients-a-communities/communities/210

Figure 6: User groups

The default setup **is the same as it was for Joomla 1.5**. If your are happy with the structure it is **not necessary to change anything**.

Default permissions for website front end user groups

- **Registered group**

    A registered user can log in, edit his own credentials and see parts of the site that non-registered users cannot see.

- **Author group**

    The author can do everything that a registered user can. An author can also write articles and modify his or her own content. There is generally a link in the user menu for this.

- **Editor group**

    The editor can do everything that an author can. An editor can also write and edit all articles that appears in the front end.

- **Publisher group**

    The publisher can do everything that an editor can. A publisher can also write articles and edit every piece of information that appears in the front end. In addition, a publisher can decide whether articles are published or not.

Default permissions for website back end user groups

- **Manager group**

    A manager can create content and can see various pieces information about the system. He or she is not allowed to:

    - Administer users

- Install modules and components
- Upgrade a user to super administrator or modify a super administrator
- Work on the menu item Site | Global Configuration
- Send a mass mailing to all users
- Change and/or install templates and language files

- **Administrator**
  An administrator is not allowed to:
  - Upgrade a user to super administrator or modify a super administrator
  - Work on the menu item Site | Global Configuration
  - Send a mass mailing to all users
  - Change and/or install templates and language files

- **Super Administrator or Super user**
  This user is allowed to execute all functions in Joomla administration. Only a super administrator can add other super administrators.

ACCESS LEVELS

User groups can be assigned to access levels. So we have a user, connected to a group, connected to an access level (*Figure 7, Figure 8*).

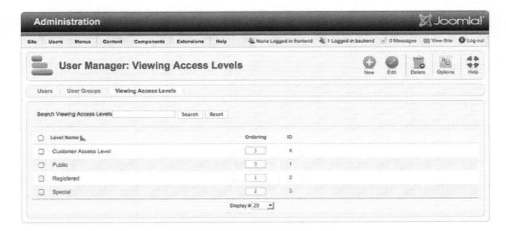

Figure 7: Access levels

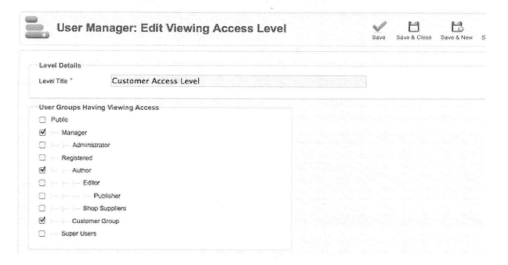

Figure 8: Groups assigned to an access level

Why access levels?

As we have seen, access levels are a bundle of groups. With the combination of group permissions and access levels it is possible to solve every use case. In an article e.g. you can limit the accessibility to an access level (*Figure 9*).

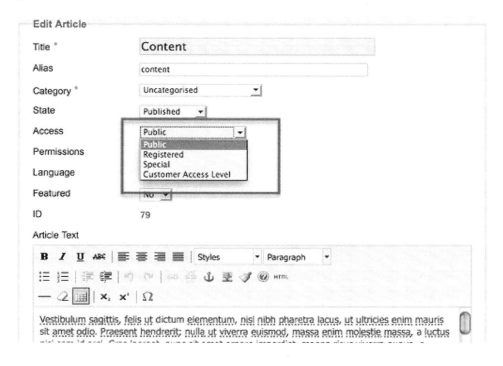

Figure 9: Access levels in an article

The new system is a big step forward for Joomla. Many users suffered from the lack of configurable groups, access level and permissions.

Such functionality is needed in order to limit access to content and functions in large organizations or to support e-commerce and subscriptions based services use cases on Joomla websites. The Joomla ACL system is not only available for Joomla content and core functions, but also available for use in Joomla extensions. For instance Community Builder and other memberships management solutions can take advantage of this enhanced ACL functionality.

USER NOTES

You are able to creates notes with review dates for each user (*Figure 10*). It is possible to group the user notes into categories. This feature allows you to setup a workflow process, e.g. for reviewing user accounts. It is possible to sort the user notes by review date (*Figure 11*).

Figure 10: User note

Figure 11: List of user notes

Mass Mail Users

Sometimes you want to send a message via email to all of your users. Sometimes you want to send that message only to a group of users or only to those having access to the backend. Sending emails is always a bit delicate. Nobody wants to be a SPAMMER and nobody wants to receive SPAM, so be careful!

In order to use the mass mail user component, you have to configure Joomla for sending emails in Global *Configuration* → *Server* → *Mail settings*. You may then configure the Subject Prefix and the Mailbody Suffix in *Users* → *Mass Mail Users: Options - Mass Mail*.

The user interface of the Mass Mail Users component is easy to understand. You can choose the user group of those users who should receive the email. Since Joomla 1.7 it is possible to decide whether disabled (blocked) users should receive the mail or not.

You can determine whether the sub user groups should also receive emails, whether the email is in html format or plain text, and whether all recipients are listed in the email or marked as BCC (*Blind Carbon Copy*). The message has a subject line and a mail body. You can use html but no wysiwyg editor is provided (*Figure 12*).

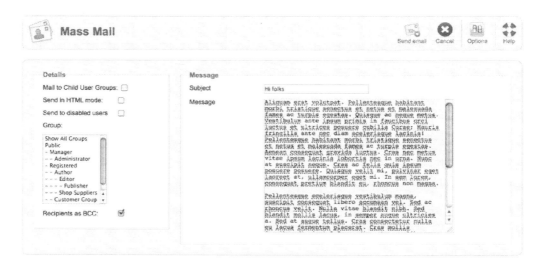

Figure 12: Mass mail form

Storing mass mails in Joomla is not possible. After filling in the form, click the send email icon. Now the emails are being sent.

Chapter 13
Extension Management

There is a lot in the core package of Joomla. Words like *components*, *modules*, *plug-ins*, *templates* and *languages* you have already heard before. Besides these well known parts, Joomla also consists of lesser known parts like *libraries* and *packages*. Additional *components*, *modules*, *plugins* and *languages* are listet in the Joomla extension directory[56]. The Joomla project has no central place for templates und libraries. The reason for this is simple. Libraries are developed outside of the Joomla project and many were also used by other open source projects. Templates are something very individual and are, therefore, available on the websites of their designers. A central directory especially for templates would be helpful in the future.

With the rewritten extension manager you can install, update, discover und manage extensions directly from your Joomla administration.

MANAGING EXTENSIONS

Let's have a look at all your installed 122 extensions in *Extensions → Extension Manager → Manager*. You can filter this list by various parameters. Some extensions are protected. Your Joomla installation would no longer work if you uninstalled these protected extensions (*Figure 1*).

---

[56] http://extensions.joomla.org/

Joomla! 2.5 - Beginner's Guide

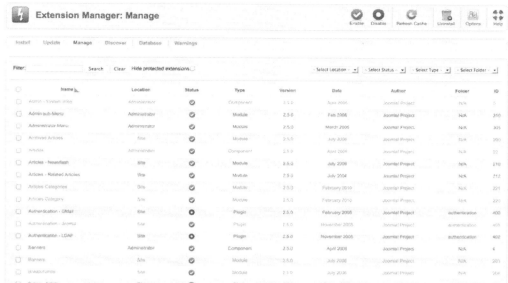

Figure 1: Table with all installed extensions

In this area you can enable, disable and uninstall extensions. Enabling and disabling works just like a light switch. You simply switch the extension on and off, all the related data are still kept. If you unistall an extension, it will be deleted. Often extensions, usually components, create additional database tables while installing. It's up to the component de-installation routines, whether these tables will be deleted or not during de-installation. Check the manual or readme file in advance to avoid suprises.

The last icon in the toolbar is the cache icon. Every extension is able to cache data. You can clear this cache separately for every extension. If your Joomla site attracts lots of visitors and you don't want to clear the whole cache for performance reasons, you may need this function.

If you filter the list for **libraries,** you will find these four articles with the corresponding version number:

- *Joomla Application Famework*, which is the real 'core' of the Joomla CMS. All the other extensions are built upon this framework.
- *PHPMailer*[57] is a class, written in PHP for sending emails. This is used in the *mail to* component.
- *SimplePie*[58] is a class, written in PHP for managing RSS ans Atom feeds. This is used in the *newsfeeds* component.

---

[57] http://phpmailer.worxware.com

[58] http://simplepie.org/

- phputf8[59] is a UTF-8[60]-capable library of functions mirroring PHP's own string functions. You can get an idea what this library does by reading UTF-8 and PHP[61].

If you filter the list for packages, you will find nothing in Joomla core. If you installed a language other than English, you will find that language package there.

UPDATING EXTENSIONS

In this area, third-party extensions and the version of Joomla core itself are listed. Here you can check for available extension updates available by clicking the *Find Updates* icon. If Joomla finds an extension update and you want to update automatically, you have to fill in the FTP setttings form in *Global Configuration → Server → FTP settings*. Then select the extension you wish to update and click the *Update* icon. The process is fully automatic and you are going to receive messages and hints, depending on the extension, while updating.

INSTALLING EXTENSIONS

You can install extensions in three different ways (*Figure 2*):

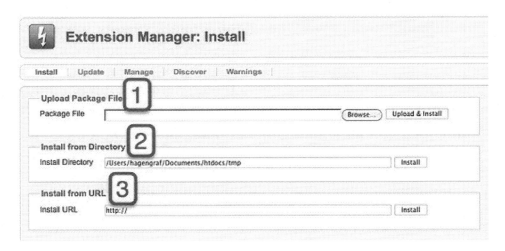

Figure 2: Installing extensions

- **Upload a Package file**
  If you have downloaded a zip file to your local PC that contains a Joomla extension, you can use this option to upload and install your extension.

---

[59] http://sourceforge.net/projects/phputf8/

[60] http://en.wikipedia.org/wiki/UTF-8

[61] http://www.phpwact.org/php/i18n/utf-8

- **Install from Directory**

  If you have uploaded a zip file at your document root directory on your web server that contains a Joomla extension, you can use this option to extract and install your extension.

- **Install from URL**

  If you know the URL of a zip file that contains a Joomla extension, you can use this option to download, extract and install your extension.

FINDING EXTENSIONS

Sometimes things are go wrong during the installation process, like files being too big, permissions not being set correctly or for other strange reasons. In this area, Joomla tries to find extensions, which are not installed but nevertheless exist in the file directory. If one or more extensions are discovered, you can install them by using the FTP feature. Don't forget the correct FTP credentials in *Global Configuration* → *Server* → *FTP settings*.

By using the discover operation, you can install multiple extensions at the same time!

WARNINGS

Error messages related to installations and updates will appear in this area. If you can't solve the problem by yourself, google the message text, you'll usually find a solution or at least some advice.

Chapter 14

Core Extensions

As we have already seen in the extension manager, the Joomla 2.5 package consists of many built-in extensions. We have already come in touch with a few of them. As a website user, you probably don't care much about the extension you are using as long as you find that it is working. As an administrator, however, you have to know exactly what is going on. We have already looked at several Joomla extensions like the *content* extension, which allows you to write and manage articles as well as publish them in different ways on the website. The *user* extension relates to users, the *category* extension to categories and so on.

In the following chapters, I am going to cover the functionality of additional extensions that are part of the Joomla core. In the *Components* menu, you will see *Banners*, *Contacts*, *Messaging*, *Newsfeeds*, *Redirects*, *Search*, *Smart Search* and *Weblinks*. We will have a look at these components including related modules and plugins.

BANNERS

The banner component provides the option to display advertising banners on your site. A banner can consist of graphics or custom HTML code. Every time your site is accessed, a different banner will be displayed from your banner administration. You can click on these banners and they are linked to the client's site. The banner component offers client, category, and banner administration as well as detailed analyses. I will guide you through a complete real life example in this chapter.

If you would like to sell advertisements on your website, there are three things you will need: clients, banners and pages on your website to display the banners. Oh, I forgot one. You also need traffic on your site. The more traffic, the better.

Depending on the contract terms you have with your clients, you may also need a tracking overview with all the impressions and clicks.

Let's begin with the client. I live in a tourist area and local businesses want to advertise their services. Joomla offers yearly, monthly, weekly, daily and unlimited subscriptions. You can configure the default subscription type in *Components - Banner – Options*.

My client would like to pay a monthly fee to appear on all pages with three different rotating banners. I add the client in *Components - Banner - Clients - New* and fill in the form (*Figure 1*).

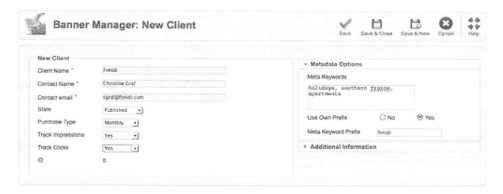

Figure 1: Adding a client

Before I can create individual banners, I have to create a banner category first. The categories are very useful because later on in the banner module, I can choose from which client and which category a banner should be displayed (*Components - Banner - Categories*).

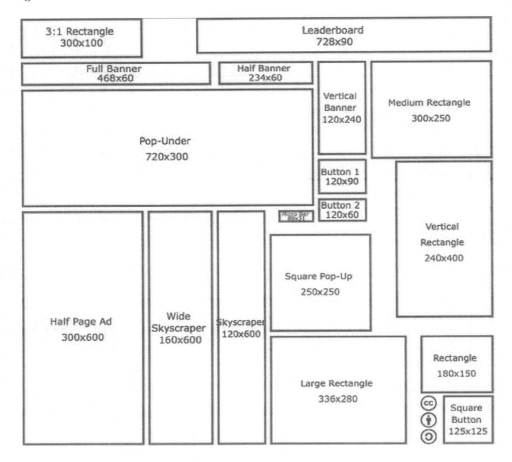

Figure 2: Standard web banner sizes[62]

 I am free to choose the size of each banner but normally you will use the standard web banner sizes. (*Figure 2*)

 The client would like to have three banners in leaderboard size (728 x 90 pixels). I'll create them in *Components - Banner - Banner*. I choose the category and the client, upload the banner and fill in the size. In *Publishing Options* I can configure several options, e.g., the start and finish date for publishing the banner. This is especially useful for time-limited subscription plans. There is also an option for re-setting clicks and impressions (*Figure 3, Figure 4*).

---

[62] http://adzaar.com/docs/standard_ad_sizes

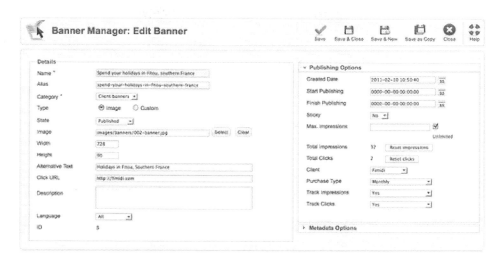

Figure 3: Adding banner form

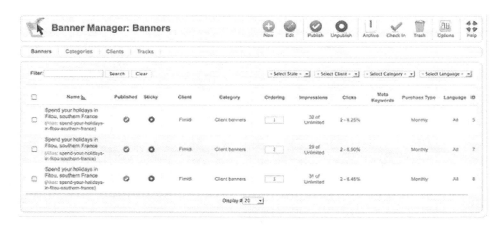

Figure 4: Banners in Administration

The next step is to create and/or activate one or more banner modules. For each banner size I need one module. In my case, all the banners are the same size, so one module will suffice. I go to *Extensions - Modules* and filter for *Banners*. At the moment there is nothing there, so I create a module by clicking the *New* icon. Depending on the template, I have to choose a position. In my case I'll choose *position 12* from the *Beez2* template. The banner will then appear above the content. In *Basic Settings* you can configure a lot more. It is also possible to show the module in your content (*Read more in chapter: Modules*).

The *Search by Tag* field is an interesting feature. When it is used, the banner will be displayed when banner keywords (set in banner) and page keywords (set in article and other places) match. Another option to control the visibility of the module and the banners is the *Menu Assignment*. One very important feature is the possibility to write a header and/or footer text. In some countries advertisements have to be labeled (*Figure 5*).

Figure 5: Banners module

The banner will now appear on the website. Depending on the configuration and the amount of banners, a different banner will appear each time you refresh the page. The banner itself is linked to the client's website and if you move the mouse across the image, a tool tip with the banner title will be shown (*Figure 6*).

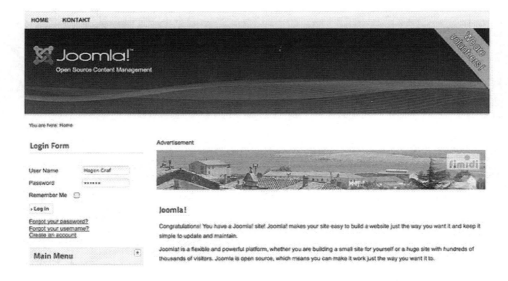

Figure 6: Banners on website

If set correctly, all impressions and clicks of the banner will now be tracked by the banner component. These trackings can be viewed in *Components - Tracks* and filtered by date, client, category and type (clicks or impressions) (*Figure 7*).

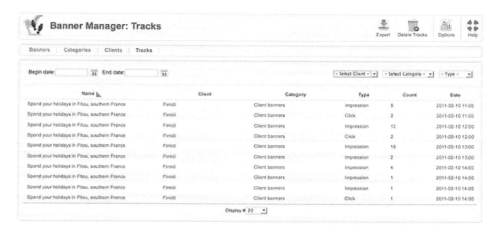

Figure 7: Banner tracking

CONTACTS

Every website needs a contact form. Depending on the provider of the website sometimes you may need only one, sometimes more of these forms. If it is a website for a company with more than one department, they may want to have a contact form for every department. Perhaps you would like to display a contact form for every employee or every user account.

All of this can be done by using the Joomla contact component.

As we have already seen (*Read more in chapter: Contact Form*), it's quite easy to set up a simple contact form. Simply create a contact, assign it to a category and create a menu item.

EXAMPLE

If several contact forms are needed, you should think about the underlying structure. Similar to article categories, it is possible to assign contact categories to menu items. As a result, you will see a list of contacts assigned to that category. If you click on the name or the title of these contacts, you will see more details and the form itself.

I have tried different scenarios with the contact component and the possibilities are amazing! As everywhere in Joomla you have the option to create nested categories and different menu item types. In options (*Components - Contact - Options*), you can, for example, configure the appearance of the contact form (*Slider, Tab, no formatting*) and set an impressive number of other parameters.

As an example I have created a contact area for our company with three contact forms for different kinds of inquiries and a contact form for each team member. By clicking on the links, the contact form and additional details will appear (*Figure 1*).

Figure 1: Contact area

For this example, I have created two categories: *cocoate* and *team*. The *team* category is a sub category of *cocoate*. It would have been possible to add an image and a description but I have decided to fill the title field only (*Figure 2*).

Figure 2: Contact categories

For each contact form I need a contact with an email address. Contacts can be assigned to users or stand alone. In this case, I have created three stand alone contacts related to the *cocoate* category without linking them to a user. I have also created two contacts related to the *team* category and additionally related to an existing user account (*Figure 3*).

Figure 3: Contacts

If any of the data changes, such as a phone number, for example, it would be nice for related users to be able to make these changes directly from their user profile on the website without having to access the administrator area. For this task Joomla provides the *User-Profile* plug-in. You just have to activate it in *Extensions - Plug-ins*. In the user profile, a new area is displayed for the profile fields, which is connected to the contact component.

Messaging

Messages is a core component of Joomla and a built-in private messaging system for backend users. It allows you to send and receive messages to other users with permission to access the administrator area.

The messaging component is very easy to use; however, users often forget the possibility to configure the component in *Components - Messages - My Settings*. You can have the system email you every new message, delete them after an x amount of days, and you can also lock your inbox.

NEWSFEEDS

Feeds are very handy. It is possible to subscribe to different kind of news and information. Unfortunately even today, often people don't use them for some inexplicable reasons. Thirty years ago you had to buy and read a newspaper to get to know the 'News'. Fifteen years ago you opened your browser and visited one website after another to get to know the "News". Today, you can still do both but it's also possible to use a feed aggregator. Google's reader[63] and the dynamic bookmark toolbar of your browser (*e.g. Firefox*) are quite popular. The Joomla *Newsfeeds* component is an aggregator as well. Not as sophisticated like Google's reader, but also quite useful.

The news feed component allows you to collect feeds from other sites and publish it on your site.

In today's world of social media everyone probably has dozens of user accounts. Often videos and images are stored on youtube.com and flickr.com. In a company, the situation is even more complex. Imagine how much information is available as newsfeeds about a project like Joomla or about your company.

A feed reader on our website

In the next example, we want to build a feed reader on our website. I'll try to collect all the bits and pieces which are created around our company and list them in a table. We have a vimeo account for our videos, a flickr account for images, several twitter accounts and that's still not all :-)

First, I create a newsfeeds category called cocoate in *Components* → *Newsfeeds* → *Categories* and afterwards for every feed an entry in *Components* → *Newsfeeds* → *Feeds (Figure 1)*. The single problem is often finding the correct feedlink. For example, our vimeo video feed link looks like this: http://vimeo.com/cocoate/videos/rss. The Flickr feed link of our photos looks more complicated (http://api.flickr.com/services/feeds/photos_public.gne?id=17963290@N00&lang=en-us&format=rss_200).

In the publishing options you have to enter how many feed entries you want to show and the number of seconds before the cache is refreshed. Joomla only stores the amount of items which you configured in its cache. This is an important detail because in some countries it is not allowed to store the content from a public newsfeed in your database.

---

[63] http://www.google.com/reader

Figure 1: A collection of newfeeds

Finally, you have to create a menu item in a menu of your choice. The *Newsfeeds* component comes with three different layouts:

1. List of all News Feed Categories
2. List of News Feed in a Category
3. Just a Single Newsfeed

I chose the second one because I have all my feeds in one category. On the website, Joomla aggregates my feeds, e.g. the Vimeo video feed (*Figure 2*)

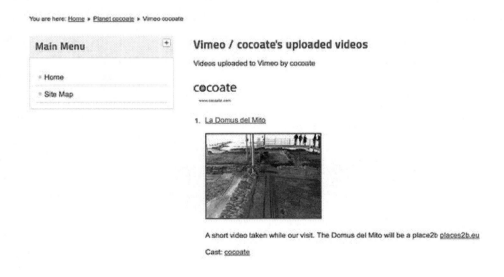

Figure 2: News feed data

When you create a news feed, you can configure in *Display Options* among other things whether you want to display the feeds image or not. Also, you can limit the number of characters of the content which should be displayed. This feature is very useful if the feed contains longer articles or if you use the *Feed Display* module. You can create one in *Extensions - Modules - New*. Here is e.g. the New York Times feed (http://feeds.nytimes.com/nyt/rss/HomePage). Configure the module at *position-4* and configure the *Basic Options* (*Figure 3*).

Figure 3: News feed module

The result on the webpage will look like in *Figure 4*.

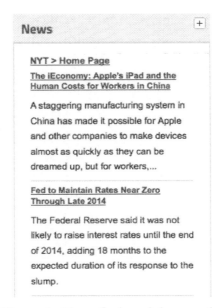

Figure 4: News feed module on website

Redirects

The redirect manager is a wonderful idea. It redirects a visitor to a valid page when he enters a path on your website that doesn't exist. It is possible that it existed before and was added to the search index of a search engine, or someone stored it at another website. This problem usually occurs after relaunching a website.

The redirect component is very convenient. If someone tries to access a path that doesn't exist, Joomla will show the *404 - not found* page and simultaneously create a new entry in the redirect manager.

When accessing *Components - Redirects*, you'll see these links (*Figure 1*). The *System - redirect* plug-in has to be activated in *Extensions → Plug-ins*.

Figure 1: Redirect Manager

Joomla! 2.5 - Beginner's Guide

You can now edit the links and add a new redirect URL. The next time the old path is accessed, the redirect component ensures that the visitor is redirected to the new address. You may create redirects on your own if you are aware of any old paths that no longer exist.

The component uses the web server's rewrite system. You have to figure out which webserver you are using. In *Site → System Information* you can see which web server you are using (*Figure 2*)

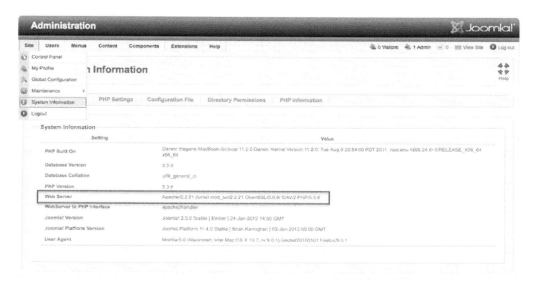

Figure 2: System Information

If your webserver is Apache, rename the file *htaccess.txt* to *.htaccess*. In some cases renaming the file may not be possible because the file starts with a dot. I use my ftp client or the shell for renaming it.

In case of using Internet Information Server rename the file web.config.txt to web.config and install IIS URL Rewrite Module before activating. (*Figure 3*).

Figure 3: .htaccess

Afterwards, go to *Global Configuration* → *Site* → *SEO Settings* → *Use URL rewriting* and switch it to *Yes* (*Figure 4*).

Figure 4: Global Configuration - Site

SEARCH

People expect to be able to search content on your website.

Joomla uses as the default setting full text search. Full text means that Joomla searches for all keywords you enter in the search box directly in the database.

This may sound obvious to most people, but it isn't. Many search engines first create a search index consisting of words used on your website. During the actual search, the search index is browsed for matches. These matches are linked to the actual content. The search result page is based on these matches and links.

Index-based search is faster than full text search but the index has to be updated with every website change; otherwise the new content cannot be found. In order to compensate for the performance advantage of the index-based search function, Joomla is highly configurable.

Since Joomla 2.5 the new core component Smart Search offers an index based search.

Search Term Analysis

To get a a first glimpse of what visitors are searching for on your site, you have to switch on the statistics feature (*Components* → *Search* → *Options: Gather Search Statistics - Yes*). Then all the terms will be recorded and listet in *Components - Search*. Don't forget to also switch on *Show Search results* (*Figure 1*).

Figure 1: Search statistics

User interface

You can choose between a search box appearing on various pages of your website or a link to a seach form. The search extension provides a search module for the single box and a search layout for menu items. The search module is activated by default and most templates provide a special search position for it. It offers numerous options, including text configuration of the buttons as well as setting the box width. One additional feature since Joomla 2.5 is the possibility to add a Joomla search to the browsers default search. The Joomla search module offers the OpenSearch Format[64] (*Figure 2*).

---

[64] http://en.wikipedia.org/wiki/OpenSearch

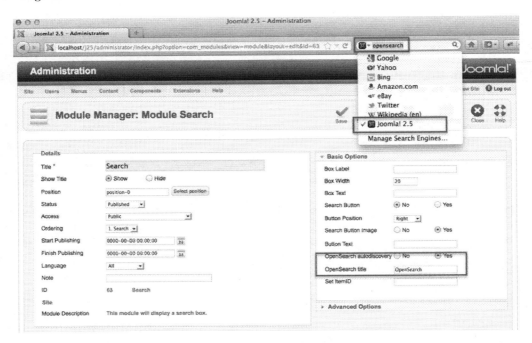

Figure 2: Search module

The search result page consists of a more detailed search form at the top of the page and the search results below (*Figure 3*).

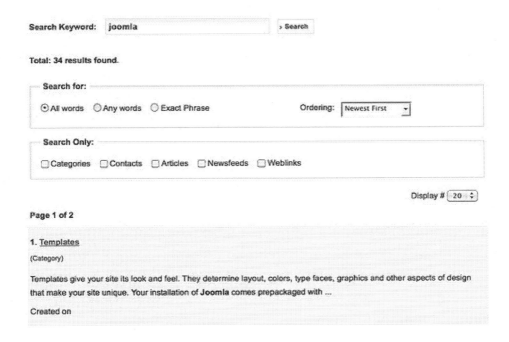

Figure 3: Search result page

The user can configure search settings (all keywords, any keywords, exact phrase) and change the order in which the results are displayed. The search can also be limited to different content items like articles and categories.

Behind the scenes

You are able to configure the search in the existing search plug-ins. Have a look at *Extensions - Plug-in Manager* and filter for type *search* (*Figure 4*).

Figure 4: Search Plug-ins

For every *search only* checkbox in the search form there is a plug-in. You can change the order of the plug-ins, activate or deactivate them. You can also configure several options for every plug-in, e.g., whether it should search in archived articles or not.

Each additionally installed extension may contain a search plug-in and integrate itself into the search process.

With this plug-in-based search structure, Joomla's search component is easy to use and easy to extend!

Smart Search

Smart Search is a new feature in Joomla 2.5.

It adds a "smarter" search engine to the Joomla core which is more flexible and faster with auto-completion and the "did you mean" feature (*stemming*).

Stemming?

> *A stemmer for English, for example, should identify the string "cats" (and possibly "catlike", "catty" etc.) as based on the root "cat", and "stemmer", "stemming", "stemmed" as based on "stem". A stemming algorithm reduces the words "fishing", "fished", "fish", and "fisher" to the root word, "fish" (Wikipedia)* [65].

The Joomla core package comes with an English stemmer and the so called *Snowball* Stemmer (*Extensions-> Smart Search -> Options*). The English stemmer works out of the box, the Snowball stemmer requires the Stem PHP extension and provides support for 14 languages including Danish, German, English, Spanish, Finnish, French, Hungarian, Italian, Norwegian, Dutch, Portuguese, Romanian, Russian, and Turkish.

The data need to be indexed in order to get this flexibility and speed.

Activation

Smart Search is disabled by default. To enable it you have to enable the Content Plug-In Smart Search and the five finder-Plug-Ins. The name finder comes from the roots of this component. It was a 3rd party component which was integrated into Joomla core (*Figure 1*).

Figure 1:Finder-Plug-in

---

[65] http://en.wikipedia.org/wiki/Stemming

INDEXING

The content needs to be indexed in order to get the Smart Search to work. This is done automatically while saving content. The initial indexing can be done in *Components -> Smart Search -> Indexing* (*Figure 2*)

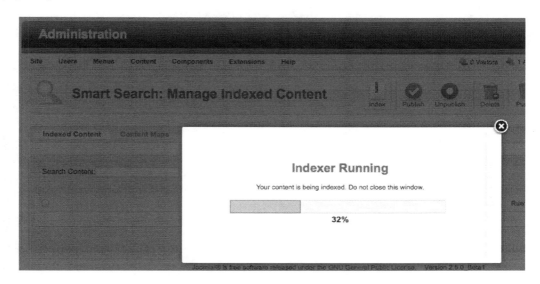

Figure 2: Indexing

CUSTOMIZING

After activation and indexing you have to decide whether you want to use the Smart Search Module and/or a Search Link in the Navigation. In both case you have the Autocompletion and the stemming (*did you mean?*) feature (*Figure 3, Figure 4*)

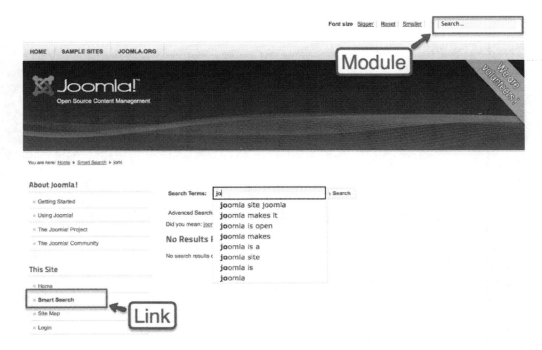

Figure 3: Autocompletion

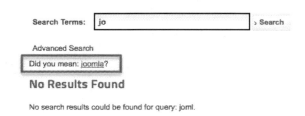

Figure 4: Stemming

You have several self explaining settings available to use predefined searches.

You find a summary in the Joomla documentation[66]

REMOVING THE CLASSIC JOOMLA SEARCH

If you decided to use Smart Search, you can remove the classic Joomla search:

deactivate or delete all module of the type search (*Extensions -> Modules -> Filter for type search*)

deactivate or delete all plug-ins of the type search (*Extensions -> Plug-Ins -> Filter for type search*)

---

[66] http://docs.joomla.org/Smart_Search_configuration_options

delete all menu links to the search component

WEBLINKS

With the web links component, you can create a link list or a download section that you can integrate into your website. To do so, Joomla provides the nested categories system and counts the individual hits on the links. This component is useful for link catalogs. Add as many web link categories as you need, create as many web links as you have, then connect both by assigning categories. Add a menu link, choose a layout and configure the options.

The web links component provides three menu item type layouts: *List All Web Link Categories*, *List Web Links in a Category* and *Submit a Web Link*. We have already seen the first two layouts in articles and categories. By using the third one, you can involve your users in the creation of a joint catalog. Create a menu item '*Submit a Web Link*' in the user menu and set the permissions in *Components* → *Web Links* → *Options* to allow registered users to create links. The *Options* area provides six tabs full of configurable details.

The example data includes a link catalog (*Figure 1*).

Joomla! Specific Links

Joomla! Home of Joomla!	4
Joomla! - Forums Joomla! Forums	4
OpenSourceMatters Home of OSM	12

Subcategories

Other Resources

Figure 1: Link catalog

In the module manager, you'll find a web links module, which shows links from a category on your website.

Chapter 15
Modules

A module is a content element that can be positioned next to an article. A menu, for example, is a module. The small registration block on the left side is also a module. You can create as many modules with smart functions as you need and position them on the predefined area in the template.

Modules are design elements in every template. Most of the time the search and the breadcrumb module have predefined positions in a template. This is also true for the navigation module in the header area, often called "top" position.

SIMILARITIES OF ALL MODULES

Every module has

- a **title** which can be displayed as a headline or hidden,
- a **position** in a template,
- a switch to **publish** the module,
- an **ordering index** for sorting modules at the same position, usually used in sidebars,
- a **scheduling feature** with a start and end date,
- the option to assign a **language** to it. Will only appear when the user selects this language (*Read more: Multi-Language Websites*)
- the option to add a **note** to the module
- the same **menu assigment** system as in templates. You can limit the appearance of the module.

ADVANCED OPTIONS

In Advanced Options, you can

- choose from different template layouts if the template offers this feature.
- add a module class suffix, which adds a text to the CSS class of the module. This is useful for individual styling.
- use the cache system by switching it on or off and set a time before the module is re-cached

CORE MODULES

Joomla! 2.5 - Beginner's Guide

    The Joomla 2.5 package contains 24 different module types. I will list and shortly describe them in alphabetical order.

    (The descriptions are partly taken from the Joomla help).

- We already used the **Archived Articles** module in the chapter Statuses, Trash and Check-Ins, which offers a list of months and is linked to the archived articles.
- **Articles Categories** displays a list of categories from one parent category.
- **Articles Category** displays a list of articles from one or more categories.
- **Articles - Newsflash** will display a fixed number of articles from a specific category or a set of categories. You can configure ordering, number of articles, read more link and many more
- The **Articles - Related Articles** module displays other articles that are related to the one currently being viewed. These relations are established by the Meta Keywords.
All the keywords of the current article are compared with all the keywords of all other published articles. For example, you may have an article on "Breeding Parrots" and another on "Hand Raising Black Cockatoos". If you include the keyword "parrot" in both articles, then the *Related Items Module* will list the "Breeding Parrots" article when viewing "Hand Raising Black Cockatoos" and vice versa.
- The **Banners** module displays the active banner, which we already used in chapter Banners
- The **Breadcrumbs** module display the navigation breadcrumbs, which were used in chapter Navigation.
- The **Custom HTML** module allows you to write your own HTML code and displays it in an appropriate module position. In *Basic Options* this module, has the usefull   *Prepare Content* feature. Joomla offers the possibility to apply additional functions to article content, like email cloaking, via the plug-in mechanism (Read more: Plug-Ins). If you turn on the *Prepare Content*, the HTML content you added to the module will be treated as any article content.
- The **Feed display** module enables the display of a syndicated feed. We used it in chapter Newsfeeds.
- The **Footer** module shows the Joomla copyright information. You are allowed to deactivate it but your are also invited to keep at on your website!
- The **Language Switcher** module is new in Joomla 1.6 - It displays a list of available content languages for switching between them. Read more about this feature in the chapter Multi-Language Websites.
- The **Latest News** module shows a list of the most recently published articles. Filtering options are: by category, author and featured articles.

- The **Latest Users** module displays the latest registered users. You can link to the user profile, limit the amount of users and you may choose between different types of user information to be shown.

- The **Login module** displays a username and password login form. It also displays a link to retrieve a forgotten password. If user registration is enabled (*User Manager* → *Options*), another link will be shown to enable self-registration for users. It is possible, for example, to add additional text to the form, to redirect your user after login and logout, and to encrypt the login form using SSL, which has to be provided by the web server.

- The **Menu** module is a container, which displays menu items of an existing menu. A menu can consist of nested menu items. You can filter these items by the start and end level, e.g., all the links from the second and third level. It is also possible to decide whether the sub menu item should be shown or not.

- The **Most Read Content** module shows a list of the currently published articles, which have the highest number of page views. You can filter by category and limit the number of articles.

- The **Random Image** module displays a random image from your chosen directory. Usually, you will use the media manager to stores these images. You can configure the file type of the image, a URL to redirect to if the image is clicked upon and you can adjust the width and the height of the images. However, be careful with the last option. Joomla does not resize the original image; it only sets attributes in the *img* tag.

- The **Search** module displays a search box. You may configure the design of the box, the position and the text of the button. We already covered the search module in chapter Search.

- The **Smart Search** is an alternative to the Search module and displays a search box. It offers, in addition to the settings of the module Search, the ability to define filters. We already covered the Smart Search in chapter Smart Search.

- The **Statistics** module shows information about your server installation together with statistics on the website users, number of articles in your database and the number of web links you provide.

- The **Syndication Feeds** module creates a syndicated feed for the page where the module is displayed. It displays the an icon. You can enter a text to be displayed near the icon and choose the feed format (RSS 2.0, Atom 1.0).

- The **Weblinks** module displays weblinks from a category defined in the Weblinks component (*Read more in chapter Weblinks*).

- The **Who's Online** module displays the number of anonymous users (e.g. guests) and registered users (ones logged in) that are currently accessing the website.

- The **Wrapper** module shows an iFrame window at a specified location. You configure the URL where the external website is located, switch scroll bars on and off, define the width and the height and give the iFrame a target name.

Joomla! 2.5 - Beginner's Guide

Chapter 16
Plug-Ins

A plug-in adds specific capabilities to a component. The term plug-in is also used in other places. For example, plug-ins are commonly used in web browsers to play videos. A well-known plug-in example is Adobe's Flash Player. A good example for the use of plug-ins in Joomla is the Search component. Five search plug-ins work together to find content from different Joomla components.

Joomla has eight plug-in types: *authentication, captcha, content, editors-xtd, editors, extension, finder, quickicon, search, system* and *user*. These are also the names of the website sub directories where the plug-in files are located. For example, plug-ins with a type of *authentication* are located in the website directory *plugins/authentication*. It is not possible and not necessary to create a plug-in in the adminstrator area like we have seen in the modules chapter. A plug-in has to be installed via the Extension Management.

AUTHENTICATION

Authentication in Joomla is the process of verifying whether a user should be permitted to do something on the site. Authorization, which is always the process that follows authentication, verifies that an authenticated user has permission to do something. You authenticate with your username and password, and you are authorized by being a member of a permission group. (read more: Users and Permissions). Joomla offers three possibilities for authentication (*Figure 1*). Be careful with deactivating plug-ins. You must have at least one authentication plug-in enabled or you will lose all access to your site.

Figure 1: Authentication Plug-ins

Joomla

The plug-in provides the standard behavior for Joomla. You fill in the login form with your username and password and your login information is then verified.

GMail

If you activate the GMail plug-in, users will be able to log onto your site by using their GMail address and password. Prior registration is not necessary. With the first login, the *System plug-in Joomla* will create a user account in its database. The GMail password is stored encrypted in the database, so your users GMail accounts cannot be hacked. This plug-in facilitates the login process for your users. Unfortunately, there is no advisory in the login form that logging in with GMail is possible. You'll have to add additional text or find another creative solution.

LDAP

The *Lightweight Directory Access Protocol (LDAP)*[67] is an application protocol for reading and editing data from directory service. It is used in companies for managing department affiliation as well as employee phone numbers.

```
dn: cn=John Doe,dc=example,dc=com
cn: John Doe
givenName: John
sn: Doe
telephoneNumber: +1 888 555 6789
telephoneNumber: +1 888 555 1232
mail: john@example.com
manager: cn=Barbara Doe,dc=example,dc=com
objectClass: inetOrgPerson
objectClass: organizationalPerson
objectClass: person
objectClass: top
```

In order to use this plug-in for authentication, you will need an LDAP Server (OpenLDAP) and you have to configure the LDAP plug-in with the server specific data. You will find a good tutorial at joomla.org: *LDAP from Scratch*[68].

Captcha

Captcha is a new feature since Joomla 2.5. A Captcha is a program that can tell whether its user is a human or a computer. You've probably seen them — colorful images with distorted text at the bottom of Web registration forms. Captchas are used by many websites to prevent abuse from "bots," or automated programs usually written to generate spam. No computer program can read distorted text as well as humans can, so bots cannot navigate sites protected by captchas. The plug-in uses Google reCAPTCHA service to prevent spammers. To get a public and private key for your domain, visit http://google.com/recaptcha. To add a captcha for new account registration, go to *Options* in the User Manager and select Captcha – reCaptcha.

---

[67] http://en.wikipedia.org/wiki/Ldap

[68] http://community.joomla.org/component/zine/article/507-developer-ldap-from-scratch-sam-moffatt.html

Figure 2: Captcha Plug-in

CONTENT

Besides the *Joomla* content plug-in, all other content plug-ins are related to the text you insert into an article. The Custom HTML can use the content plug-ins as well (*Figure 3*).(Read more: Modules)

Figure 3: Content Plug-ins

Smart Search

The plug-in enable the indexing of content. It is a feature since Joomla 2.5 and the base for the Joomla Smart Search.

Joomla

The Joomla plug-in has two tasks:

1. When you attempt to delete a category, it verifies whether the category is 'empty'. Empty means, no article or sub category is assigned to it. You can turn this feature off in *Basic Settings*.

2. If a new article is submitted via the frontend, the plug-in will send an email to all those users for whom *Send Email* is turned on (*User Manager - Edit User*). This feature can be turned off in *Basic Settings*.

Loading Modules

This plug-in loads the HTML output of all modules assigned to a template module position into an article. All you have to do is write *{loadposition position-14}* in the space where the modules should displayed. This feature is especially useful for putting banner ads into the content.

Email Cloaking

This plug-in transforms an email address entered into the content in the form of name@example.com into a link, and cloaks the email address by means of JavaScript. The advantage of this is that email address collection programs can't read your email address very easily.

Code Highlighter

The GeSHi plug-in makes *Syntax Highlighting* possible and creates an impressive listing on your website if you embed the code to be formatted within *<pre> </pre>* HTML tags:

```
<pre>
if ($number > 0)
{
  echo $number;
}
else{
  $number++;
}
</pre>
```

Pagebreak

The Pagebreak plug-in takes care of pagebreaks in articles. Just like the *Image* plug-in, it is easy to integrate into the content. Besides a simple pagebreak, various headers and page titles can also be defined. You can set pagebreaks using the pagebreak dialog. The page break will be displayed in the text window as a simple horizontal line. In the HTML code, the pagebreak looks like this:

```
<hr title="Page Title" alt="Table of Contents Alias" class="system-pagebreak" />
```

This plug-in integrates the *Next* and *Previous* functions under the articles.

Page Navigation

This plug-in integrates the *Next* and *Previous* functions under the articles.

Vote

This plug-in adds voting functionality to articles.

EDITORS

Joomla core comes with two editors (*Figure 4*). In *Global Configuration - Site* you can set the default editor for your website. Additionally, you can assign a different editor to every user account (*User - Manager*).

Figure 4: Editor Plug-ins

CodeMirror

CodeMirror[69] is a JavaScript library that can be used to create a relatively pleasant editor interface for code-like content — computer programs, HTML markup, and the like. This plug-in has to be activated if you want to offer textarea fields with the CodeMirror editor. You can configure the behavior of the editor in *Basic Settings*.

None

This plug-in has to be activated if you want to offer textarea fields without an editor.

TinyMCE

TinyMCE[70] is a platform-independent web-based Javascript HTML WYSIWYG editor control. It is the default editor in Joomla

EDITORS-XTD

The four editors-xtd plug-ins generate the buttons below the editor window (*Figure 5*).

---

[69] http://codemirror.net/

[70] http://tinymce.moxiecode.com/

Figure 5: Editor-xtd Plug-ins

Article

Displays a button for linking the actual article to other existing articles. After clicking the button, a pop-up will be displayed allowing you to choose the article to link to.

Image

This plug-in displays a button for inserting images into an article.
After clicking the button, a pop-up will open allowing you to choose an image from the media directory or upload new files and configure its properties.

Pagebreak

Provides a button to enable a pagebreak to be inserted into an article. A pop-up allows you to configure the settings to be used. The plug-in has to be activated together with the *Content - Pagebreak* plug-in.

Readmore

Enables a button which allows you to easily insert the *Read more* link into an article.

EXTENSION

The extension plug-in type is related to tasks concerning the managing of Joomla extensions.

Joomla

This plug-in manages the update sites for extensions.

FINDER

The Smart Search component was formerly Finder. That is the reason for the name of this plug-in type. The Smart Search plug-ins for Contents, Weblinks, Contacts, Categories, and Newsfeeds can be activated when needed. They implement the search function of the Smart Search component. These plug-ins have to be activated if you are trying to obtain search results from the respective sections. If you want to search additional components, the respective plug-ins for those have to be available as well (*Figure 6*).

Figure 6: Smart Search Plug-ins

QUICKICONS

The plug-ins of this type are checking for updates for Joomla and for your installed third-party extensions and notifies you when you visit *Site -> Control Panel*.

Figure: 7 Quickicons

SEARCH

The Search plug-ins for *Contents*, *Weblinks*, *Contacts*, *Categories*, and *Newsfeeds* can be activated when needed. They implement the search function of the Search component (*Read more in chapter Search*). These plug-ins have to be activated if you are trying to obtain search results from the respective sections. If you want to search additional components, the respective plug-ins for those have to be available as well (*Figure 8*).

Figure 8: Search Plug-ins

SYSTEM

System plug-ins are deeply integrated in the Joomla framework, and they usually affect the behavior of the entire website (*Figure 9*).

Figure 9: System Plug-ins

Language Filter

This plug-in filters the displayed content depending on the language desired. It has to be enabled only when the *Language Switcher* module is published (read more in chapter: Modules)

P3P Policy

The *Platform for Privacy Preferences Project (P3P)*[71], is a protocol allowing websites to declare their intended use of information they collect about browsing users. The system P3P policy plug-in allows Joomla to send a customized string of P3P policy tags in the HTTP header. This is needed for the sessions to work properly with certain browsers, i.e. Internet Explorer 6 and 7.

Cache

This module provides page caching. You can configure whether you would like to use the client's browser for caching pages.

Debug

This makes the debug function available, which is very important to programmers. You can configure the parameters to determine which information to display.

Log

This plug-in makes the system log files available.
You can determine the location of the log file in *Global Configuration - System - System Settings*.
This is an example of such a log file (*/logs/error.php*):

```
#Version: 1.0
#Date: 2011-07-06 12:39:38
#Fields: date      time      level     c-ip      status    comment
#Software: Joomla 1.7.0 RC1 [ Ember ] 28-Jun-2011 23:00 GMT
2011-07-06 12:39:38 - 92.143.161.32 Joomla FAILURE: Empty password not allowed
```

Redirect

Provides the redirect feature in conjunction with the Redirects component.

Highlight

This plug-in highlights specific terms and is used e.g. in the Smart Search component.

Remember Me

This is a method for saving access data locally in a cookie in the client browser. Once a user visits your website again, the data is already in the form. This storage is only enabled by explicitly marking a checkbox below the login form.

SEF

SEF is the acronym for *Search Engine Friendly*. This plug-in creates search engine friendly URLs for content elements, which can be configured in *Global Configuration - SEO Settings*.

---

[71] http://en.wikipedia.org/wiki/P3p

Logout

The system logout plug-in enables Joomla to redirect the user to the home page if he chooses to logout while being on a protected access page.

Language Code

The Language Code plug-in provides the ability to change the language code in the generated HTML document to improve SEO.

USER

User plug-ins are related to user specific functions (*Figure 10*).

Figure 10: User Plug-ins

Profile

The user profile plug-in gives you the opportunity to ask the user for additonal profile fields, which can be configured in *Basic Settings*. It can also be combined with the contact creator plug-in to automatically create a contact item for every user (*also see chapter Users and Permissions*).

Contact Creator

A plug-in to automatically create contact information for new users. It works in conjunction with the profile plug-in (*also see chapter Users and Permissions*).

Joomla

This plug-in creates a user in the database after the first successful authentication.

Chapter 17
Working with Templates

To be able to work with templates, you will not only need good design skills but also have an understanding of HTML and CSS. Some browsers, unfortunately, will not display the latest versions, which is why other versions are still quite common.

The next challenge is the never ending discussion between developers and designers about 'how to do things the right way'. Designers depend on developers because they need HTML markup with a possibility to add CSS classes. Developers also depend on designers because without a well-designed template the best component will be difficult to use.

Joomla has built-in solutions for both challenges!

The Beez Template also exists as an XHTML and a HTML5 version and the suitable HTML markup and CSS classes are created with so-called *Overrides*. *Overrides* means that a designer can override the HTML output the developer's extension produces, without changing the original source code.

Another important agent in the template industry is 'Joe Webmaster'. Often, he only wants to change the header graphic, the colors, the width and a few other options.

Joomla again has the perfect solution for doing this and it is called *Template Style*. *Template Style* means that you can create any number of copies of an existing *Template Style* to configure your own set of options and assign it to all or various menu items. Have a look back at the chapter Templates and come back for a deeper insight.

CREATE YOUR OWN STYLE

In the chapter about Multi-Language Websites, we built a website based on the *Beez2* template. Now I would like to create my own style and change a few options in *Extensions - Template Manager - Beez2 default*. These changes are as follows:

- *Style name:* Beez2 - cocoate
- *Logo:* I do not want a logo, so I click the *Clear* Button
- *Site Title:* Joomla
- *Site Description:* cocoate - consulting, coaching, teaching
- Template color: Nature

I save the style as a copy by clicking the *Save as Copy* icon (*Figure 1*).

Figure 1: Individual template style

My website now has a totally different look (*Figure 2*). It is possible to create different styles for different parts of the website using the menu assigment feature.

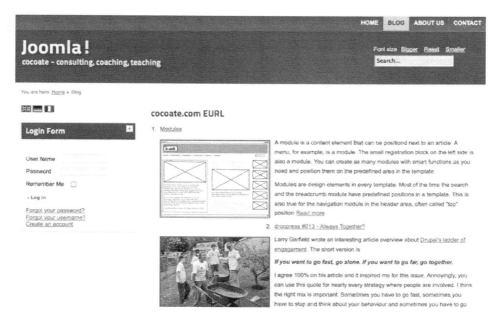

Figure 2: Website with Beez2 style

Creating different styles with available options is the easiest solution and often the best and fastest. When a Joomla update becomes available, your individual styles will still be accessible in the new version. You are still working with the core package of Joomla 2.5 without any additonal extensions!

Customizing Existing Templates

If you are reading this chapter, I assume you have already created a *template style*, figured out how to work with all of the available template options, but would still like to have more possibilities. Welcome to the world of HTML and CSS! I'll also assume that you know these two abbreviations. If not, have a look at wikipedia for HyperText Markup Language (HTML)[72] and Cascading Styles Sheets (CSS)[73].

In Joomla it is possible to edit all CSS used by the template within the Joomla template manager. Go to *Extensions - Template Manager - Templates* and click on the link *beez_20 Details*. There, you will be able to make changes in the *beez2* template as well as access all modifiable files (*Figure 3*).

Figure 3: Beez2: Customize Template

The editable CSS files are the files that are located in the file system in the folder *htdocs/templates/[template_name]/css*. Click on the linked name of the CSS file and a form will open, in which you can edit the file content by using the *CodeMirror* editor. Besides the CSS files, you can also edit the three main template files:

- **Main page**

htdocs/templates/[template_name]/index.php

- **Error page**

If an error occurs while opening a Joomla site, this template is used for the page.
htdocs/templates/[template_name]/error.php

---

[72] http://en.wikipedia.org/wiki/Html

[73] http://en.wikipedia.org/wiki/CSS

- **Print view**
  This template is responsible for the output when you access the print view.
  htdocs/templates/[template_name]/component.php

More template pieces like the files for the *core overrides* are located in *htdocs/templates/[template_name]/html*. The *core overrides* cannot be edited from the administrator backend.

The changes you make here will change the core *Beez2* files. This is something to keep in mind in case of updates.

Overrides

You have already created a style, changed the CSS files and the main page of your template and you are still unhappy with the result? :-) Then this is the perfect time to discuss overrides. In Joomla there are two kinds of overrides: *template overrides* and *alternative layouts*.

Template overrides

Let's assume you want to change the layout of the search result page. A component like the search component has a default template layout, which is stored in the file */httpdocs/components/com_search/views/search/tmpl/default.php*. This file makes the search page look the way it looks. Add a few words to the file, save it and you will immediately see the result! For example, add

```
<strong>I have changed something :-) </strong>
```

in line 13 and see what happens (*Figure 4*).

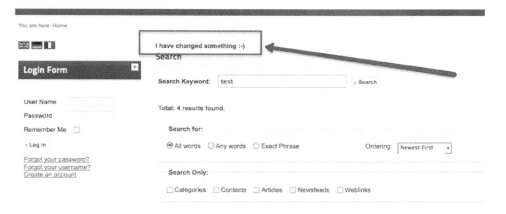

Figure 4: Changes in the HTML output

The result is good for your motivation because it was so easy and is displayed in every template. However, **it is not good for your reputation because you have just changed core code**. With the next Joomla update, your changes will be gone!

A better alternative would be to use *template overrides* in each template. Copy the changed file to your template folder to */httpdocs/templates/[template_name]/html/com_search/search/default.php* and remove the changes in the original file. The result on the webpage is the same but, behind the scenes, you have overridden the original *.../default.php* file with your desired content layout - without changing core code - well done!

This system was introduced in the year of 2007 with the release of Joomla 1.5 and still works very well today.

Alternative layouts

In Joomla 2.5 the overrides have an enhancement called *alternative layouts*. I am sure you have already seen the *Alternative Layout* field in the edit form of articles, modules and categories (*Figure 5*).

Figure 5: Alternative layout in an article

Why do we need alternative layouts? Imagine, you are an administrator or webmaster and a template comes with three alternative layouts for an article. Sometimes it is a 'normal article', sometimes it should look like a product, and sometimes like a book page. You only have to choose which layout you would like to use. That sounds like a great feature and, of course, it is.

The technique is the same as with template overrides. You have to create a folder with the same name as the component or module and a subfolder for the view. There are two differences:

1. Obviously the file name has to be something other than *default.php* as this one has already been reserved for template overrides.

2. The alternative layout is, of course, not automatically selected.

Additionally to the alternative layout, menu item types can be added to the layout and the option items of that article can be controlled by defining them in an xml file with the same name as the alternative layout file (*Figure 6*).

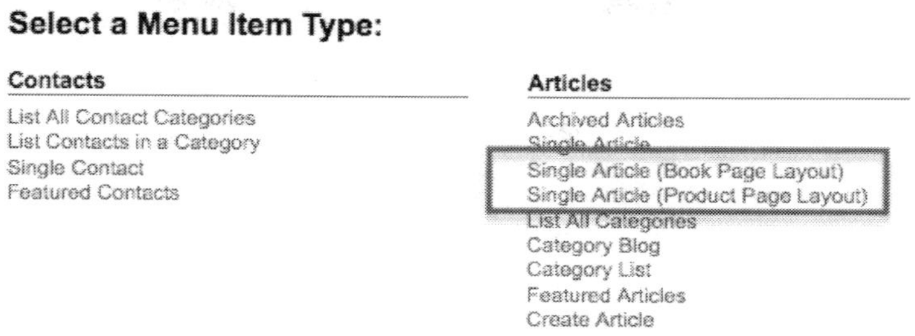

Joomla! 2.5 - Beginner's Guide

Figure 6: Additional menu item types

The creation of these files are no beginner's topic but I am sure third-party templates will soon make use of these new possibilities (*Figure 7*).

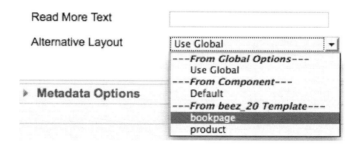

Figure 7: Additional layouts in an article

CREATE A NEW TEMPLATE USING ATOMIC

The Atomic template is a skeleton for your own template. It consists of:

- /htdocs/templates/atomic
  component.php - the print view template
  error.php - the error page template
  favicon.ico - the website icon (*Favicon* [5])
  index.html - a security file displaying a blank page when the directory is entered directly (also has to be configured by the webserver but usually is)
  index.php - the templete main page
  templateDetails.xml - The configuration file containing all information about files, options and positions is necessary to show the template in the template manager and to later create an installable zip package.
  template_preview.png - the template preview image, displayed in template manager
  template_thumbnail.png - the template thumbnail image, displayed in template manager

- /htdocs/templates/atomic/css
  the folder for CSS files

- /htdocs/templates/atomic/html
  the folder for *Override* files - Atomic provides a few *Overrides* for modules.

- /htdocs/templates/atomic/images
  the folder for images

- /htdocs/templates/atomic/js
  the folder for Java script files

- /htdocs/templates/atomic/languages
  the folder for language files - Atomic comes with English base language files.

Main template file index.php

The file name of this layout file has to be *index.php* since Joomla searches for embedded <*jdoc*> and PHP commands. All necessary HTML markup is already built-in and commented. You can change the content of the file according to your needs.

To get an idea, let's do a quick walkthrough:

In *line 24* you can choose whether you want to use the blueprint CSS framework or not.

In *line 50, 56, 62* and more you see that the template provides positions with special names (*atomic-search*, *atomic-topmenu*, ...). If you want to use these names you have to assign your modules to these positions. If you want to change the names, you may do that in the *templatedetails.xml* file.

In *line 24* you will see:

```
echo $this->baseurl ?>/templates/<?php echo $this->template ?>/js/template.js
```

Joomla knows the values in *baseurl* as well as the name of your template and you can access them when needed.

In *line 46* you will see:

```
echo $app->getCfg('sitename');
```

It will tell you the name of your site.

In *line 48* you will see:

```
if($this->countModules('atomic-search')) ...
```

It counts the amount of modules at the position *atomic-search*. It is used to adjust your layout to different situations.

In *line 50* you will see:

```
<jdoc:include type="modules" name="atomic-search" style="none" />
```

This is a <jdoc> command, which only exists as a name space in Joomla. It is used to insert the HTML output of the given type into the attributes. In this case it means the output of all modules assigned to the template position *atomic search*. The style attribute is called *module chrome* and can have these values

- **table** - The output is displayed in a table.
- **horz** - The output is displayed horizontally in a cell of a surrounding table.
- **xhtml** - The output is in in an XHTML-compliant <div> element.
- **rounded** - The output is in a format in which round corners can be displayed. The class of the element is renamed from *moduletable* to *module*.
- **none** - no formatting
- **outline** - the display type for the position preview (*?tp=1*)
- **Template specific style** - Some templates, like Beez, have their own styles. See chapter The Beez Template.

You will find a complete list of styles in the Joomla documentation - *What is module chrome* [6].

Other <jdoc> types are:

```
<jdoc:include type="head" />
<jdoc:include type="message" />
<jdoc:include type="component" style="none" />
```

Every page needs a *head*, sometimes a *message* (after saving) and, of course, a *component*. One *component* can be displayed per page. The *component* can make use of the module chrome as well. The *error* and the *print view* template files work exactly like the *main* template file.

CSS Folder

You will find three files in this folder.

1. The css/*template.css* file with predefined commented CSS commands. If you don't use the blueprint framework, you have to uncomment a few of them. The lines are specifically marked.

2. The file css/*template_ie.css* is empty. Here you can add style overrides for Internet Explorer.

3. The file css/template_rtl.css is empty as well. You can add style overrides for right to left languages.

Blueprint framework

Blueprint is a CSS framework designed to reduce development time and ensure cross-browser compatibility.

A few sentences taken from the *readme* file:

> Welcome to Blueprint! This is a CSS framework designed to cut down on your CSS development time. It gives you a solid foundation to build your own CSS commands. Here are some of the out-of-the-box features BP provides:
> * An easily customizable grid
> * Sensible default typography
> * A typographic baseline
> * Perfected browser CSS reset
> * A stylesheet for printing
> * Powerful scripts for customization
> * Absolutely no bloat!

You will find demos and tutorials on the project website - *http://www.blueprintcss.org/* .

Chapter 18

Angie Radtke
The Beez Template

A template usually contains more than you see at first sight.

The term template is usually connected with the visual appearance of a website. But in addition to the design, it is distinguished by the way of the technical implementation. It determines where the content is located within the flow of documents, when and where certain modules can be switched on and disappear, whether custom error pages are used and what markup - version of HTML should be used.

Some users will certainly be familiar with the Beez template in Joomla 1.5. Both, *beez_20* and *beez5* are visually very different from the design of the previous version. For the design I used a neutral grey for the elementary components of the template, such as the menu to provide a solution that harmonizes with many colours.

Even at that time, I wanted to develop a standard compliant, easily accessible and adaptable template. I consciously had chosen the colour purple, in the hope that many designers would take the code, modify it and make it freely available. I had hoped for a variety of many new free templates. This has unfortunately not occurred.

Another mistake was probably that I did not communicate clearly enough what the real aim was. The output was structured in a way so that almost any design could be implement in a simple and straightforward manner, with only slight modifications in the CSS. I kept this principle in the new versions of Beez. Additionally, there is a more accessible JavaScript and in beez5 a small portion of HTML5[74]. *Beez_20* does not require template overrides. Layout tables are finally not in use anymore in Joomla. The new HTML-based output follows the structure of the old Beez template.

The CSS class names have been renamed and unified for a better understanding. This is a tremendous advantage for template designers. The HTML output from the Joomla Standard is clean and well-formed. You do not need to use template overrides anymore to generate clean, standard-compliant code. The technical capabilities of both Beez templates are almost identical. They differ only in their graphic design. The *Beez5* version is also designed for the use of HTML5.

- Accessibility

---

[74] http://en.wikipedia.org/wiki/HTML5

- Configurable position of the navigation
- WAI-ARIA Roles Landmark
- Automatic representation of the modules in accessible tabs
- Fade in and out of collapsible modules
- Fade in and out of collapsible column
- In *beez_ 20* you can choose between two forms: natural or human
- In *beez 5* HTML5 is usable

GENERAL ACCESSIBILITY

For most people the Internet has become the norm. Information from around the world are ready for retrieval and perhaps, more importantly, also the special offers at the local hardware store, the opening times of the registration office or the phone book are available on your home screen. Annoying phone calls or library visits are unnecessary, you just look on the net.

But not everybody benefits from this development. Those people, with any physical or mental disability have difficulties to participate fully in society, even though they could benefit enormously from communications technology. But they often fail because of barriers that obstruct their access to information or make it even impossible. Many of these barriers can be overcome, if the offers are designed accordingly.

Operators of online shops or banks which provide Internet banking, should be aware of that not so small target group.

Accessible web design aims at making content and interactions on the Internet accessible for all user groups and devices, if possible.

Approx. 8% of the German population have a physical limitation that makes it difficult for them to access information from the Internet. Commonly the term "accessibility" in web design is identified with Internet for blind people. I want to emphasize that this is not all - indeed, this is only the smallest part. I've often wondered why this is so. Probably the reason is that the monitor has become the classic symbol for the computer, and someone who sees nothing, cannot use it. In my daily work, I have noticed that even blind people cope much better than people with other types of disabilities.

Blind are people whose residual vision is only a few percent of the average value. The number of blind people in Germany lies between 150,000 to 200,000. Some of them can decipher just texts through the computer font size and customized colour settings, while others depend on acoustic information or read by touching the Braille display.

Significantly greater is the proportion of people with severe visual impairment.

About a quarter of the population in working age complains of various degrees of ametropia. Later on, the percentage is much higher. Some of these problems can be compensated by glasses quite well, others with limitations only. Certain eye diseases such as cataract or glaucoma can be resolved or at least mitigated through surgery. Some, like retinitis pigmentosa or diabetic retinopathy, lead to a steady deterioration of vision and ultimately often lead to complete loss of vision. "In the so-called" tunnel vision, the visual field of the affected people is extremely limited - sometimes to the size of a two-Euro coin, which is held at arm length from the eyes.

About 10% of the male population is affected by mild forms of colour blindness – which usually means that some reds and greens cannot be distinguished from each other. Blind to other colours, complete colour blindness or red-green colour blindness in women are very rare.

One other potential group of users has problems with the usual input technology - not everyone can use a mouse or a standard keyboard.

There can be many reasons: arms and fingers are immobile or move spontaneously and are difficult to control. Others have even no arms and no hands or are paralyzed from the neck down after a stroke on one side. As long as a human being is capable to send a controlled binary signal - the famous 0 or 1 – he can learn to operate a computer and its functions with appropriate software.

There are about 60,000 to 100,000 people in Germany with extremely limited ability to hear. Several thousand of these were disabled in learning the German language so that they know it only imperfectly (at the level 4th to 6th grade). This makes the demand for more understandable texts clear.

To communicate with each other, but also for the reception of foreign or sophisticated content they prefer the German sign language - this is an idiom on its own, independent of the spoken language based on a system of signs and gestures.

Attention

Not only people with low hearing abilities surf the Internet without or with speakers turned off! It is not sufficient, for example, to give acoustic warning signals only - they must always be accompanied by a clearly interpretable visual notice.

The more the Internet conquered all areas of life, the more situational disabilities are visible: slow connections in the hotel, uncontrollable lighting conditions in the moving train, arranged waiver of sound in the workplace.

All people benefit from accessible websites. It is not about meeting all the rules to the fullest extent, which governmental institutions are required to comply to. Even small steps toward accessibility can significantly improve the usability of a website.
Due to its high penetration, Joomla has the ability to influence a lot. With the standard template beez it is now relatively easy, to create websites which are accessible and usable for many.

As in beez 1.5 all those things that are necessary for the design of accessible templates are implemented also in beez_20 and beez5. The most important are:

- Separation of content and layout
- Semantically logical structure
- Anchors links
- Keyboard navigability
- Sufficient colour contrasts

Separation of Content and Layout

The first and most important rule for developers is the possible complete separation of content and layout:

- Clean and pure HTML for the content
- No unnecessary layout tables
- Formatting exclusively with CSS
- A logical semantic structure
- Anchor links

The linearisable issue of content and formatting via CSS only is one of the most important conditions for convenient accessibility.

Only then assistive technology has the option to recycle the contents at will, while the visual presentation can be completely ignored. The outsourcing of the presentation in style sheets give, for example, visually impaired users, the possibility to define own style sheets in their browser and adapt that the pages exactly fit his/her needs. A linear presentation of content and an adequate semantic structure is particularly important for users of screen readers.

Screen readers grasp the content of a site from top to bottom, that means linear. The use of extensive layout tables hinders linearisation.

Behind the term Semantic Web probably most of the people can imagine only very little. You probably associate language lessons, but it also plays a special role in writing Web content. For example, screen readers offer their users to jump from heading to heading or from list to list, to get a quick overview of the overall document. If a Web document has no headers, this functionality is not available.

The formal structure of a web document should largely correspond to the content structure. Depending on the Web project the choice of the corresponding heading hierarchy can be quite a challenge.

Today, this concept can be found not only in the templates, but in the entire Joomla Standard output. In the development of Joomla 1.6, this was a central part of the development work. Reasons were, in addition to better usability in assistive technologies, also search engine optimization and better usability in mobile devices. Well-structured code not only helps people with disabilities better navigate within a site, even Google feels better with such a well-structured site.

Anchor Links

Linear presentation of content has a big drawback: You may have to travel a very long way, in order to access *"in the back lying"* areas of content.

On the screen, a three-column layout allows that a number of areas begin *"above"* and the eye can jump right to it, where it, supported by visual aids, suspects interesting information.

Remedy offers the concept of anchors. It is, in fact, a non-visual counterpart to the graphical layout and allows the user of linear playback devices to identify key content areas at the beginning of the page and then immediately jump to the area where he/she believes the information of his/her interest lies.

Practically, the use of anchors means, to set up an additional menu at the top of each page for internal navigation of the page. In most cases it will be useful to hide this menu from the graphical layout. It's irritating for users, that can see, to click a link, but nothing (apparently) is happening, because the link target is already visible in the viewport.

In any case, the *"anchor links menu"* should be not too long and built in a very well thought-through manner, because it extends and complicates, due to the linearisation itself, the path of perception. In general, it's advisable to offer the main content as the first target jump, then regular visitors, who know the site and handle the navigation specifically, have the shortest way to where they actually want to go to.

At least here it becomes clear that, particularly websites with more complex content pages do not only need a graphical layout, but also a content design that aims to arrange the content in a form that it contains no unnecessary barriers for the users of linearising clients.

Example:

```
<ul class="skiplinks">
  <li><a href="#main" class="u2">Skip to content</a></li>
  <li><a href="#nav" class="u2">Jump to main navigation and login</a></li>
</ul>
```

The Colour Choice

The colour choice is, in the context of accessibility, of particular importance because even people with impaired colour vision should be able to use your website fully.

If you convert to a layout into shades of gray, you gain an approximate idea of what colour-blind people can see. However, the perception is very individual and depending on the severity of different degrees of ametropia. Many colour-blind people, however, have learned during their life, what colours are represented by what they see. They know, for example, that grass is green, and they can identify by comparison and other shades of green.

Much more widespread than the total colour blindness is the so-called red-green colour blindness. Affected by a genetic anomaly, people are not able to distinguish the colours red and green. Mixed colours that contain these colour components are blurred for them.

Contrasts

Colours also play an important role in various other types of visual impairment, not only because of the colour itself, but also a significant colour contrast can be helpful in the use of a web page.

Foreground and background colour within the text elements should form a distinct contrast, though it is not possible to select the colour and contrast settings, which can meet all requirements. Black text on white background achieves a maximum colour contrast. To avoid disturbing glare effects, a slight tinge of the background can be useful. Some visually impaired people will need very strong contrasts to separate the individual elements of content in a page from each other. For them, colour combinations such as white text on a bright, contrasting orange background are not rich enough. In contrast, other strong contrasts act as a radiation - the content is difficult to read.

BEEZ_20: DESIGN CHOICE

In the Beez 2.0-Template, you can choose between personal and nature design. The implementation of the files *nature.css* and *personal.css* via the template parameters as well as the structure of the used CSS files are the basis for this method.

Figure 1: Choose the Style

There are two more files which are responsible for the colour scheme. The *position.css* and the *layout.css* are responsible for the overall positioning and spacing.

Would you like to change later only the colours of the template, you can simply modify the files personal.css or nature.css as desired. The positioning of the content remains the same, as they are defined in other files.

All style templates are still arbitrarily modifiable and can be amended by template developers to include additional templates.
In the design of the source code I have taken into account to offer the maximum possible creative variations by modifying the CSS files. I'm telling you that very, very quietly, but in their own way, the Beez templates are something like frameworks and save you a lot of working steps.

POSITION OF THE NAVIGATION

For aesthetic reasons or to improve the search engine friendliness and accessibility, it may be necessary to position the navigation before or after the content. Both versions of the Beez templates let you choose between two options in the backend.

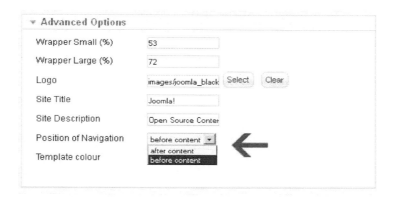

Figure 2: Select position of the navigation

The navigation is visually and semantically positioned before or after the content and formatted by use of CSS.

If you open the *index.php* of *beez_20* or or the template you have already modified, you can find around line 27 the following assignment:

`$navposition = $this->params->get('navposition');`

The variable *$navposition* is assigned to the currently selected value in the backend. The variable expels the value *left* or *center*. *Left* represents the position before the content, *center* stands for the positioning after the content.

The term *center* seems to be a little confusing here, it would be logically better to say it is *right*. But depending on how you design the CSS, you can place the navigation in three-column view in the middle.

JAVASCRIPT AND WAI ARIA

WAI-ARIA (Web Accessibility Initiative - Accessible Rich Internet Applications) is a technical specification of the Web Accessibility Initiative[75], which will facilitate the participation for people with disabilities in today's increasingly complex and interactive web services. This technique is particularly helpful in designing dynamic content presentations and user interfaces. The technique is based on the use of JavaScript, Ajax, HTML, and CSS.

Especially blind people often lose orientation when visiting a site where content is suddenly displayed or hidden. People, that can see, can sense this change with the eyes, blind people can understand it only when the focus is placed on the item.

To focus means nothing else than to place the cursor in the appropriate place to make the positioned content accessible.

In HTML and XHTML we did not had the opportunity to focus on all elements. Only the interaction elements such as links, buttons or input fields were focusable. This has changed with the use of WAI ARIA and HTML5.

The used scripts within the Beez templates rely on this technique to make the template accessible to people with disabilities.

WAI ARIA - LANDMARK ROLES: FIRST AID FOR THE ORIENTATION

Landmark Roles are intended to facilitate the orientation on a website by describing page areas and their exact function within the page. The navigation has the role navigation, search has the role search, the main content has the role main. The implementation is quite simple. The element is extended only to the appropriate role attribute. Thus, users of modern screen readers will be informed of this role.

```
<div id="main" role="main">
```

Inside the Beez template, this is done automatically by using javascript *(javascript/hide.js)*. The approval of the Wai-Aria technology is still pending and with the direct implementation into the source code the website would fail doing the validation test.

A complete overview of the landmark roles can be found at http://www.w3.org/TR/wai-aria/roles#landmark_roles.

If you later use the Beez template as the basis for your own template and modify the structure of page areas, you should adapt the script accordingly.

Collapsible modules and sidebars

---

[75] http://en.wikipedia.org/wiki/Web_Accessibility_Initiative

The activation and deactivation of certain areas can be helpful for the user, especially on pages with a lot of content. Both Beez templates provide two different ways. First, the column with additional information can be fully switched on and off, on the other hand, the modules can be collapsed up to their headlines.

Hide Column

To test this functionality, you have to place a module in the column for additional information. The module positions *position-6, position-8* and *position-3* are available. No matter whether the navigation is before or after the content, whenever this column is displayed, a link appears right above with the text *"close info"*.

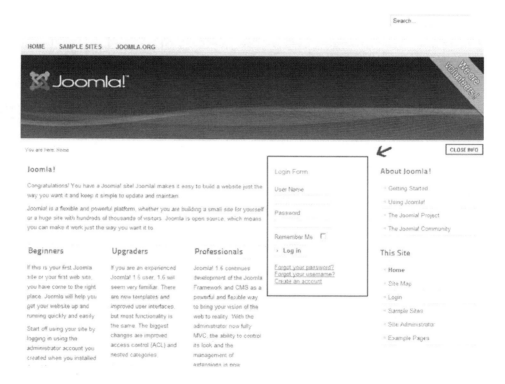

Figure 3: Hide Column

By activating this link, the column is hidden, the link text will change to "open info" and the column will be re-activated by clicking.

This functionality is controlled by JavaScript. All the scripts mentioned here are based on the supplied Mootools JavaScript framework that diminishes our work in many areas.

The file *hide.js* in the JavaScript folder of the template is responsible for showing and hiding the column.

In the *index.php* of the template, around line 194, you will find the necessary HTML code.

```
<div id="close">
 <a href="#" onclick="auf('right')">
  <span id="bild">
   <?php echo JText::_('TPL_BEEZ2_TEXTRIGHTCLOSE'); ?>
  </span>
 </a>
</div>
```

The textual contents of the JavaScript variables are controlled with the Joomla language strings.

Show and hide modules

One of the biggest challenges in designing a website is the clear structuring of the content. Especially on the homepage, you often need to place a variety of information without cluttering the page.

Figure 4: beez-Slider

Both Beez templates have the opportunity to present modules in the form of sliders.

Here, the first output is the title of the module. By clicking on the plus sign next to the heading, the module opens and its contents will be visible. Then, the plus sign replaced by a minus sign and the module can be folded back. Even with this method I have used the WAI ARIA technology.

In order to use modules as described, they should be integrated in the template by using the command.

```
<jdoc:include type="modules" name="position-8" style="beezHide" headerLevel="3" state="0" />
```

By using the *style = "beezHide"* all modules that are loaded at this position are shown as sliders.

You may have noticed that the command includes the attribute "state", which controls whether the module is expanded or collapsed.

If you choose the value 0, it is closed when it first loads, select the value 1, it is opened by default and can be closed by the user.

Accessible Tabs

The presentation of content in so-called Tabs is becoming increasingly popular. There are already modules that Joomla extends with this functionality. But none of the offered modules fulfilled the requirements of accessibility.

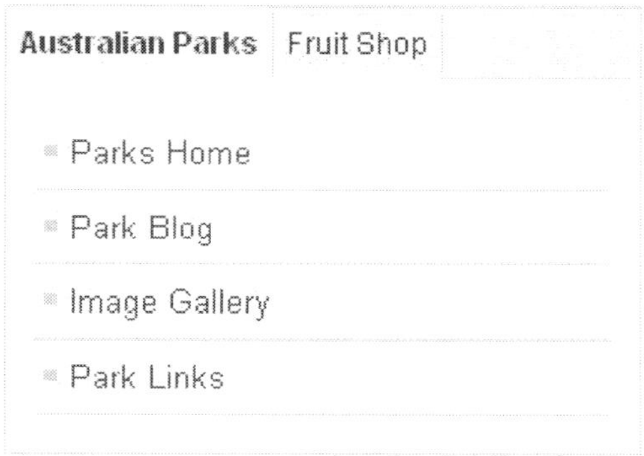

Figure 5: BeezTabs

The integrated solution in Beez is based on the WAI-ARIA techniques to ensure accessibility. To represent the modules in tabs, they are integrated as follows.

```
<jdoc:include type="modules" name="position-5" style="beezTabs" headerLevel="2" id="1" />
```

All on the *position-5* placed modules are arranged automatically in the form of tabs. You control the HTML output via the Style beezTabs. The use of the attribute *id = "3"* is mandatory. The reason lies in the structure of the used JavaScripts. Imagine, you want to integrate modules at different places into your template. The JavaScript function requires a unique information about where which tabs should be opened and closed. If this information is missing, the script will not work as desired. Please use at this point numbers only for the id.

ADJUST FONT SIZE

In the top head of the layout the user is able to change the font size. The technical basis for this function can be found in the JavaScript file *templates/your_name/JavaScript/md_stylechanger.js*. Within the index.php you include a div container with *id="fontsize"*.

This area is initially empty and will then be filled dynamically with content using JavaScript. If your visitors should have turned off JavaScript, this function is not available.

Some might be asking, why this function is still necessary, as every browser has a feature to increase font size. Especially for older people this technique is often of particular importance, since most of them have a more or less impaired vision. However, particularly older people often know very little about the functionality of web browsers and look forward to an apparent offer.

BEEZ5: USE HTML5

The *Beez5* template is hardly different from *beez_20*, apart from some design aspects. The features offered are largely identical.

The only difference: *beez5* allows the use of HTML5. If you take a look at the template parameters of *beez5*, you see that you can choose between HTML5 and XHTML code output. This is based on the HTML5 template overrides, which you find in the HTML folder of your template.

HTML5 provides a variety of new possibilities and will bring a number of changes and easements in the future, but it is still not yet an approved standard (March 2011). Many of the options offered are currently not reliably applicable, but others can already be used without difficulties.

A very important part, which already works, are the new structuring elements. HTML4 and XHTML had low semantic weight. This has improved significantly with HTML5.

We have now really practical elements to structure the page.

With the elements

- header
- footer
- aside
- nav

you can structure a wonderful page.

Elements such as

- section
- article
- hgroup

help you to assign more importance to the actual content.

The HTML5 code in *Beez5* uses only the elements that are reliable right now. Only the *Internet Explorer Version 8* has some problems, as always.

In the top of the page a script is inserted, which integrates the unknown elements in the existing document structure.

```
<!--[if lt IE 9]>
<script type="text/JavaScript" src="<?php echo $this->baseurl ?>/templates/beez5/JavaScript/html5.js"></script>
<![endif]-->
```

Basis for the integration of HTML5 in Joomla are the template overrides and the response to the selected markup language via the template parameter in the index.php. Because the template allows the use of two different markup languages, you have to approach this possibility in the *index.php*.

Clearly said: The construction of the *index.php* is quite complicated, because depending on the selected markup language another HTML code is generated.
It starts with defining the type of document.

When you open the index.php of *Beez5* templates, you can instantly see what I mean.

```
<?php if(!$templateparams->get('html5', 0)): ?>
<!DOCTYPE html PUBLIC "-//W3C//DTD XHTML 1.0 Transitional//EN" "http://www.w3.org/TR/xhtml1/DTD/xhtml1-transitional.dtd"><?php else: ?>
<?php echo '<!DOCTYPE html>'; ?>
<?php endif; ?>
```

This concept is carried through the whole page and the HTML5 elements can only be issued if HTML5 was also selected in the backend.

If you later want to build your own template in HTML 5, it would be better you remove all the queries and XHTML elements and output directly the HTML 5 code.

Chapter 19

Written by Milena Mitova

Why SEO is important for you

As a website owner, developer or builder, you know that getting web visitors is key to a successful web presence. In a world where the Internet rules and the fastest way to learn new things, locate the right products and services, or find user feedback is to use search, you have to follow the established online search practices if you want to be found by the people who are looking for the likes of what you are offering on your website. To give you an idea of how powerful online search has become in recent years, below are a few numbers provided by ComScore[76], a research company specializing in digital marketing intelligence:

- Google searches: 88 billion per month
- Twitter searches: 19 billion per month
- Yahoo searches: 9.4 billion per month
- Bing searches: 4.1 billion per month

JOOMLA 2.5 AND SEO

As one of the most advanced Open Source content management systems in the world, Joomla has been designed to provide you with all the features and functionalities that you need to make your website search engine friendly and ready to be found by your right audience. As you probably know, the process of

> *"improving the visibility of a website or a web page in search engines via the "natural" or unpaid ("organic" or "algorithmic") search results"*[77]

is called SEO or Search Engine Optimization.

The two main functions of SEO are to drive traffic consisting of high-intent visitors ready to become prospects or customers, and to help build your online brand.

---

[76] http://www.comscore.com/Press_Events/Press_Releases/2010/1/Global_Search_Market_Grows_46_Percent_in_2009

[77] http://en.wikipedia.org/wiki/Search_engine_optimization

SEO has on-page and off-page elements, which you can review in detail in this very useful infographic[78] by searchengineland.com. The great news is that Joomla can help you with both of these elements, enabling you to build a solid SEO foundation that can be easily extended into a successful traffic-driven web presence.

SEO FUNCTIONALITIES INCLUDED IN JOOMLA 2.5
SEO-friendly Urls

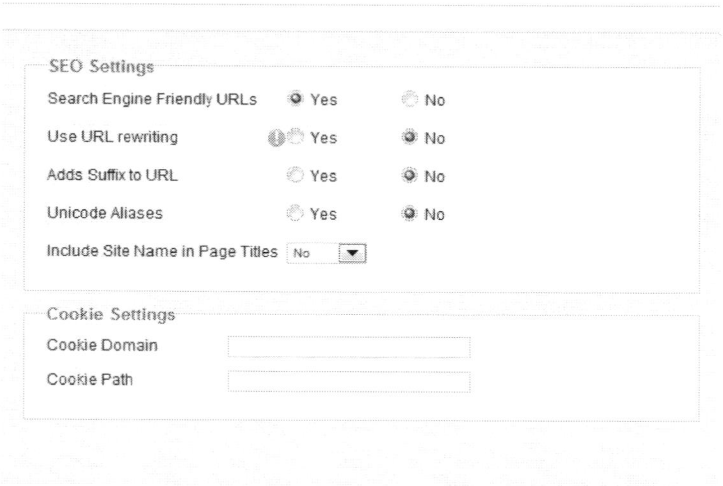

Figure 1: Figure 1: SEO-friendly Urls

According to Google's Matt Cutts[79], the best website urls consist of not more than 3-5 words. From that point on, the longer the urls, the less ranking power they will have.

This is how your urls will look once your Joomla site is set up:

> http://www.yourdomain/index.php?
> option=com_content&view=article&id=8:beginners&catid=19&Itemid=260

And this is how they will look after you have modified your access.txt[80] file and switched on the SEO url feature, accessible in Joomla's Global Configuration control panel:

> http://www.yourdomain/products/your-product-name

---

[78] http://searchengineland.com/seotable/

[79] http://www.mattcutts.com/

[80] http://www.teachmejoomla.net/joomla-mambo-tutorials-and-howtos/general-questions/how-to-enable-seo-on-joomla.html

Search engines can read the first type of urls, called dynamic urls, without any problems. However, it is common practice to use the second type, called SEO-friendly urls, instead. There are two reasons for this:

1. Users tend to click more on url links that make sense and have relevant search words

2. Dynamic urls are very often the culprit in what search engines might interpret as duplicate content, which in turn can affect negatively your page rankings in search results.

Joomla allows you to set up your SEO-friendly urls in two easy steps - by editing the Global Configuration on the admin back-end and by making a few minor changes to the access.txt file that resides in the root folder of your server. You can additionally modify the actual words that each url contains by editing that in the article text editor of your content or in your menu item setup panel.

SEO Browser Page Titles

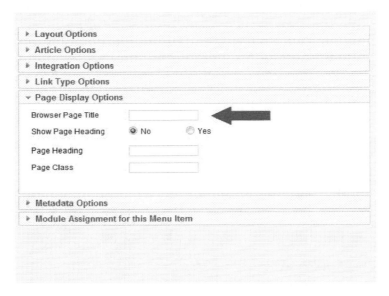

Figure 2: SEO Browser Page Titles

Title tags, also referred to as "Browser Page Titles" in your admin backend (they are usually displayed at the top of a browser's window) are the most important SEO elements that directly affect the ranking of your individual pages. To be effective, each title has to be:

- Unique for each page,
- Extremely relevant to the content on that page,
- 70 characters long, max,

- Should include the key search word you are optimizing the page for.

This is how it works, as explained by seo.com[81]:

> "For example, let's say you have an educational site that provides information and guidelines on teacher certification requirements. You've decided that the most important keywords for your site are "teaching certification" and "teaching requirements." In this case, a page title along the lines of "Teaching Requirements for Teacher Certification" is highly relevant to the topic of the site. Spiders will crawl your site, and because the title is the first factor it sees, the spider will "read" it and then examine the rest of the page finding the keywords used in other places on the page to determine how relevant the title is to the rest of the content. If the content, H tags, and title tag all relate—you're in business! This is why it's so important to target the most critical keywords in the title tag."

With Joomla, adding the title tags is an easy and hassle-free process. You can add and modify the tags of all of your pages from the menu item setup panel.

SEO Meta Descriptions for All Your Pages

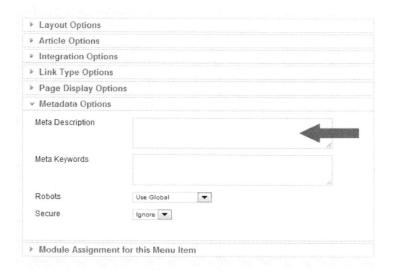

Figure 3: SEO Meta Descriptions for All Your Pages

Meta description is the brief summary that shows up under the url of each individual result that a user sees in the search results page after performing an online search query. While it is no longer considered of key importance as far as search engine rankings are concerned, it defines how successful

---

[81] http://www.seo.com/blog/seo-tips/title-tag-seo-tips/

your click through rate is (i.e. whether or not users will actually feel compelled enough to click on your page link). Meta descriptions shouldn't be longer than 160 characters.

Figure 4: SEO Meta Descriptions in Search Engine

Joomla enables you to add meta descriptions to all of your pages – even when you are creating a page that displays a whole category of articles. You can manage this process on two levels – at the menu-item level (for category pages) and at the article level (inside the text editor where you write your article) (*Figure 3*).

Easy Image Titles for SEO

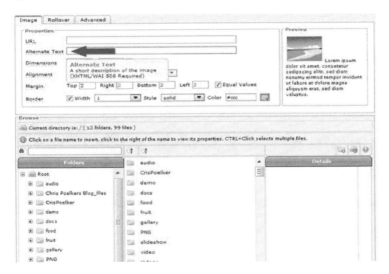

Figure 5: Image Titles for SEO

Search bots are not able to see images correctly. This is where the "alt" tags or image descriptions/titles come into play. They help make your images searchable, ultimately helping with your SEO. Joomla provides you with an easy-to-fill image dialog box[82], where you are conveniently prompted to include a

---

[82] For more information: http://www.joomlacontenteditor.net/

short description for your image. This is one more easy-to-use SEO enhancing feature that can provide quick and relevant results.

Redirect for SEO Best Practice

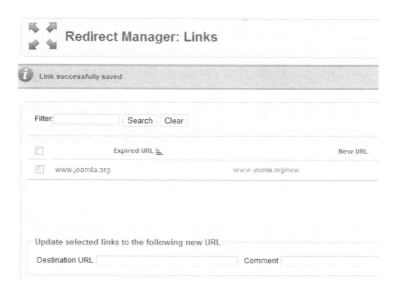

Figure 6: Redirect Manager

In his article about Redirects and SEO[83], Stephan Spencer, an SEO expert and blogger says the following:

> *"Use of the proper kind of redirects is a matter of SEO "best practice". Every site needs to have redirects (e.g. for example, from your non-www version of your site to your www version or vice versa). And if you don't, you're leaving money on the table. In addition, sites evolve over time and URLs change. And any time you make changes to your URLs — whether it's to the domain, subdomain, subdirectories, filenames, or query strings — you need to ensure links pointing to the old URLs are still valued by Google and the other engines, and that their voting power gets transferred to the new URLs. "*

Redirecting users from your old or non-existing pages, documents and other website assets to your new ones can be done in 3 easy steps using Joomla's native redirect component. It is user-friendly, has zero learning curve, and the best part about it is that every time a web visitor hits a non-working page, the component lists the problem url, as well as how many times it was clicked on. You can then swiftly fix the problem by adding a new url to redirect future visitors to a page that works.

---

[83] http://www.stephanspencer.com/redirects-and-seo-best-practic

RSS for better SEO

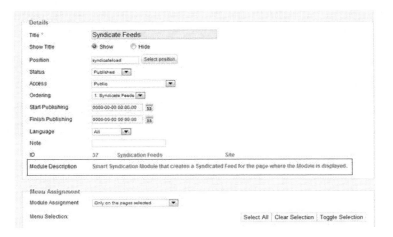

Figure 7: Feeds Module

RSS will enhance your SEO efforts by helping you build more backlinks. As you know, the more backlinks you have to your site, the more Google and the other search engines will trust it and push it up in the search ranking results. The simplest way to use RSS for SEO purposes is to use Joomla's syndication feeds module to set up RSS feeds for your content and post the feed links on your website and social media channels (LinkedIn, Facebook, etc.), as well as on some of the various content aggregator sites that exist on the web, like feedage.com, etc. You can also share your RSS links with partners and other non-competing sites – as long as you constantly provide relevant and fresh content, many organizations might be willing to subscribe to and display your feed on their website, thus helping you build more backlinks.

IN CONCLUSION

Using all of the features highlighted above will provide a fast and easy way for you to establish and maintain the right SEO practices for your website. However, result-driven SEO is not just about titles and images. It starts before you even begin to build your site and is an on-going project that needs to be managed regularly and measured for success. Here are a few great resources that I would like to recommend. They will help you learn everything that you need to know to become your very own free and effecive SEO consultant:

This is a very useful 8-part training series on keywords[84] by wordtracker.com, which is free. It introduces you to the concept of keywords and explains why SEO starts with defining your main,

---

[84] http://www.wordtracker.com/academy/keyword-basics-part-1-how-search-engines-work

category and page keywords, helping you understand how to find your best keywords and how to include them in your texts in order to build a steadily-growing, free, organic traffic to your site.

To learn more about SEO and the way to implement it, read this searchengineland.com's free step-by-step Guide to SEO[85].

This is another article that offers a quick 5-step guide to jump-starting your do-it-yourself SEO program[86].

The SEO Cheatsheet by SEOMoz[87] gives you great tips on getting your SEO processes up and going in no time.

The Web Developer SEO Cheatsheet by SEOMoz[88] is a great infographic, showing you how you have to structure content on your page.

---

[85] http://searchengineland.com/guide/seo

[86] http://magazine.joomla.org/topics/item/403-5-Quick-SEO-steps-that-will-help-you-get-better-rankings-and-more-traffic-to-your-Joomla-site

[87] http://static.seomoz.org/user_files/2006/seomoz-cheatsheet.swf

[88] http://static.seomoz.org/user_files/SEO_Web_Developer_Cheat_Sheet.pdf

Chapter 20

Multi-Language Websites

I live in Europe. The European Union has 23 official languages. If you are going to create websites in regions like this, you have to think about multilingualism. Two things are especially challenging when it comes to creating multi-language websites: the translation of the static Joomla text strings as well as the translation of the content items. While the first challenge can normally be overcome easily, the second one presents the real challenge.

The Joomla 2.5 core is available in more than 40 languages languages and more languages are expected to come soon.

Let's build a multi-language website by using Joomla 2.5 core in this chapter.

JOOMLA LANGUAGE PACKAGES

You can download the translation packages from Joomla Code[89] or the Joomla extension directory[90] und install them using the extension manager (*Read more: Extension Management*). I have done this with the German as well as the French language package. After installation you will find the three installed languages (*Figure 1*) by visiting *Extensions → Language Manager* in the backend.

Figure 1: Installed languages (EN, DE)

Language Configuration

As of now, it is still necessary to have a look at the language configuration to see whether the languages are published (*Extension → Language Manager → Installed*) and the language content attributes

---

[89] http://joomlacode.org/gf/project/jtranslation1_6/frs/

[90] http://extensions.joomla.org/extensions/languages/translations-for-joomla

are correct (*Figure 2*). Have a look at (*Extension → Language Manager → Content*). If there is no content item for the installed language, create one by clicking the new icon. This is what happened to me after I had installed the French language package.

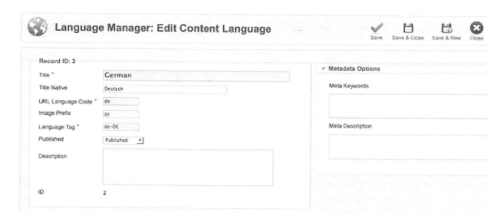

Figure 2: Edit content language

LANGUAGE FILTER PLUGIN

For Joomla to be able to distinguish between the different languages, the *System - Language Filter* plug-in (*Extensions → Plug-Ins*) has to be activated. You are able to configure the language to be shown to the visitor, whether it is the language version of your website or the client's browser setting, by simply using the Options settings. Another configuration setting is the *Automatic Language Change*. If enabled, the content language will automatically be changed to the frontend language settings.

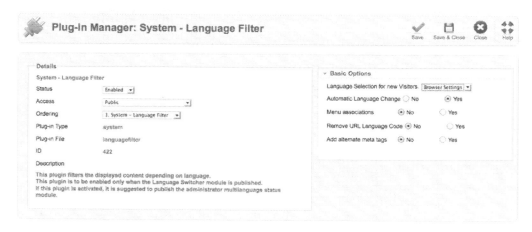

Figure 3: Plug-In - Language Filter

Every user can configure his *frontend language* once he is logged in in the frontend. Most of the time, there is a user menu that, depending on your rights, provides you with different menu items. In this user menu, you will also find the *Your profile* link. By clicking on the link, you will then be able to view and edit your profile data. In the profile edit form under *Basic Settings*, users can choose among other configurations and set their *frontend language* (*Figure 4*). You may use the default website language or one of the available content languages. Depending on these settings, the language plug-in will allow you to view the website in the corresponding language.language.

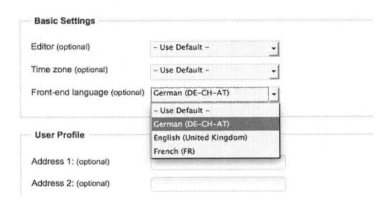

Figure 4: User profile - Basic Settings

LANGUAGE SWITCHER MODULE

By activating the *Language Switcher* module, you have the possibility to switch between languages in the frontend, regardless of whether you are a visitor or a logged in user. In Basic Settings you can add text and choose whether you would like the languages to be displayed with the language name or the flag icon. I am sure some third party templates will provide special templates positions for this module in the near future. In the default template *Beez2*, *position-7* works well in combination with the flags.

Joomla! 2.5 - Beginner's Guide

Figure 5: Language Switcher

It is important to read the description text careful (and twice)

> When switching languages and if the menu item displaying the page is not associated to another menu item, the module redirects to the Home page defined for the chosen language.
> Otherwise, if the parameter is set for the Language filter plugin, it will redirect to the associated menu item in the language chosen. Thereafter, the navigation will be the one defined for that language.
> If the plugin 'System - Language Filter' is disabled, this may have unwanted results.

Method:

1. Open Language Manager Content tab and make sure the Languages you want to use in contents are published and have a Language Code for the URL as well as prefix for the image used in the module display.

2. Create a Home page by assigning a language to a menu item and defining it as Default Home page for each published content language.

3. Thereafter, you can assign a language to any Article, Category, Module, Newsfeed, Weblinks in Joomla.

4. Make sure the module is published and the plugin is enabled.

5. When using associated menu items, make sure the module is displayed on the pages concerned.

6. The way the flags or names of the languages are displayed is defined by the ordering in the Language Manager - Content Languages.

If this module is published, it is suggested to publish the administrator multilanguage status module.

MULTI-LANGUAGE CONTENT ITEMS

As I have previously mentioned, each content item, such as an article, can be assigned to a language. The difficulty now lies in creating all these content items in all source and target languages (*Figure 6*). You can create content items in any language but, unfortunately, Joomla 2.5 does not yet offer a translating workflow, which means that you have to pay attention to avoid mistakes.

Figure 6: Language field

You can create content items in any language but, unfortunately, Joomla 2.5 does not yet offer a translating workflow, which means that you have to pay attention to avoid mistakes.

A MULTI-LANGUAGE WEBSITE

My example website consists of

- a front page with articles,
- a blog,
- an 'About Us' page,
- a contact form.

Figure 7: Example website

All content items have to be available in different languages (*Figure 6*).

Front page

I create a few articles for each language with the attribute featured (*Read more in chapter: A Typical Article*)

To make it easier for you to start I created a screencast (will be published soon for 2.5). This is the 1.7 version (which still works)[91]

I create a menu called default with a menu item called *default*, which links to *Featured Articles*. I configure this menu item as *Home* by clicking the *Home* icon. The menu *default* needs no corresponding module, it should simply exist (This behaviour is in the actual version of Joomla 2.5 and will hopefully be changed in the upcoming updates).

Afterwards I create a menu per language and the corresponding menu module. I create a menu item for each language : (*Home*, *Startseite*, *Accueil*). These menu links have to be configured as Home by clicking the *Home* icon (*Figure 8*). If you see the flag beside the menu item, everything works fine, if not ... watch the screencast :)

---

[91] http://vimeo.com/28593435

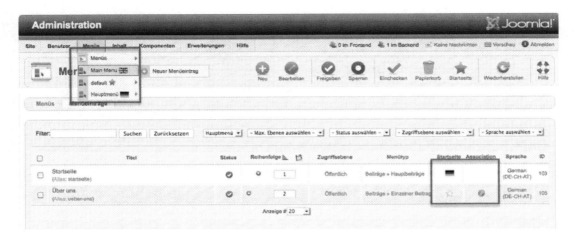

Figure 8: A frontpage for each language

A blog

In my case I already have a blog at cocoate.com, so I use the newsfeeds component for displaying the external blog entries. I create a feed item for each language and the corresponding menu items (*Read more in chapter: Newsfeeds*).

An 'About Us' page

I create an 'About Us' page as described in chapter How to create an 'About Us' Page for every language.

A contact form

I use a single contact form for genaral inquiries. I only need one contact item, so it is not necessary to assign a language. Only if contact data differs in different languages, e.g., different address or email, will it be necessary to create one contact item for each language.

Login form

On each page a login form will be visible. I have copied the English login module twice, configured the menu assigment, changed the title and assigned the correct language. Now it is possible to login and register at my site.

User menu

I used the existing user menu, which provides you with a link to your profile as well as for creating an article or weblinks. (*Figure 9*).

Figure 8: Front-end editing

As you can see, creating a multi-language website with core Joomla is quite simple!

LANGUAGE OVERRIDES

If you notice language strings that are not appropriate to your website you can change them in Extensions -> Language Manager -> Overrides.

> *A language string is composed of two parts: a specific language constant and its value.*
> *For example, in the string:*
>
> *COM_CONTENT_READ_MORE="Read more: "*
>
> *'COM_CONTENT_READ_MORE' is the constant and 'Read more: ' is the value.*
> *You have to use the specific language constant in order to create an override of the value.*
> *Therefore, you can search for the constant or the value you want to change with the search field below.*
> *By clicking on the desired result the correct constant will automatically be inserted into the form.*

You can search for these language strings and overrides them by filling the formwith your customized texts (*Figure 10*).

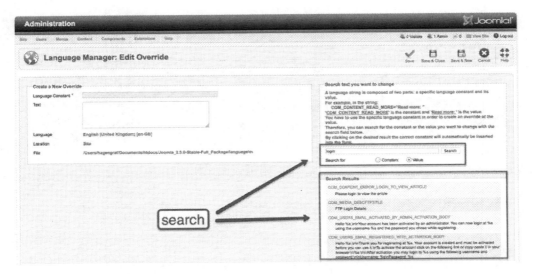

Figure 10: Language overrides

Chapter 21

written by Jen Kramer

A Joomla 2.5 Website from Scratch

FIRST, START WITH A PLAN

There are two kinds of website builders.

The **first** is all too typical. A client asks,

> I'd like a website, and I want it blue; how much will that cost?

The builder responds,

> If you get it with a calendar, it will cost X, or you can also get it with a blog for Y.

This kind of builder serves as a button-clicker. The client asks for something, and rather than applying analysis or years of experience to the problem the client needs solve, this builder simply delivers a site the way the client requested it.

The **second** kind of website builder has a future with bigger clients in it. When asked the same question, this builder says,

> Sure, we can definitely make your website blue. Can you tell me about your organization and what you hope your website will do for it?

By asking instead about a client's organization and the problems they need solved, you will be developing a relationship of trust with your client. That means completing the site is the start of the relationship with your client, leading to further work, rather than the completion of your relationship with the client. It's much easier to get continuing work from existing clients, rather than continuously seeking new ones.

Assuming you want to be the second, more successful website builder, here are some pointers for putting together your Joomla 2.5 site from scratch.

Goals of the organization, users, and website

Start a discussion with the client about their organization, whether it's a business, a non-profit, or a personal website. You might ask some of the following questions, and there are many additional questions to these:

- What is the goal of the organization? (Examples: end world hunger, make money by selling knitting products, provide updates about my latest activities)
- When was the organization founded and who does the organization serve?
- Why does the organization need a website? Does a website already exist, or is this a new site?
- If a site already exists, what is worth keeping in the old site? What would you add to the content of the old site? Is the site's message still on target, or has the organization changed since the last site design?
- Who will be maintaining the website? (Examples: IT staff, in-house webmaster, the secretary in addition to other duties, or the organization sends its updates to you to complete)

You will likely want to ask many additional questions to these above to fully understand your client and the answers to the following three key questions:

- What are the goals of this organization?
- What are the goals of the website, and how does it support the goals of the organization?
- What do the site visitors want from the website, and how does that fit with the goals of the website and the organization?

Out of this discussion, you should identify some extension types you'll need to include on your site (for example: a calendar with an "upcoming events" module; a blog with comments and tagging; a shopping cart that interfaces with PayPal).

You should also develop a site map for your website. This is a detailed description of all pages on your site and how they link together. The term site map also refers to a page on your site containing links to every page on the site. The first site map you create is spelling out all of the pages and navigation structure on a piece of paper, and the second site map can be generated by an extension like XMap.

For more information on website planning, I recommend the following resources:

- The Elements of User Experience[92], by Jesse James Garrett
- "Website Strategy and Planning"[93], lynda.com video training, by Jen Kramer

---

[92] http://www.amazon.com/gp/product/0321683684/

[93] http://www.lynda.com/Interactive-Design-tutorials/websitestrategyandplanning/53259-2.html

Next, consider the technology

If you are reading this book, and particularly a chapter called "A Joomla 2.5 Website from Scratch", I assume you have chosen Joomla for building this website.

Clients may wish to know why you've chosen Joomla for the site, or why it's a good choice of technology for them. Some arguments I use when selling Joomla include:

• Joomla is one of the top three open source content management systems [94] in the world, backed by a thriving community and an active development process. New releases of software occur every six months.

• Joomla powers over 23.5 million sites worldwide[95], and it is the choice of over 3000 government sites.

• Because Joomla is open source technology, the client is not tied to a single web development firm, the way they would be with proprietary software. There are many firms available to help with your site.

• Joomla's interface is easy to use, and clients love the ability to make changes to their site without involving a web developer.

It's unlikely you'll use just Joomla's core to build your website. In most cases, you'll want to add some third party extensions to your website. A great place to start looking for these is the Joomla Extension Directory[96] (JED). Debating which Joomla extensions are "best" or "critical" to each website is a topic of conversation that never seems to get old among Joomla designers and developers.

Do not stack your Joomla site with endless extensions. It's best to pick a minimum number of extensions, just the ones you need most, and don't load the site up with unneccesary additional technology. Each extension should address a purpose identified as part of the goals development process described above. Just because you can put in extra extensions because they're "cool" or you think they're interesting to use does not necessarily mean they should be used on the site, unless they contribute to reaching a site goal.

Now you're ready to build

With a plan established and extensions selected, and your site map in place, you are ready to assemble your Joomla website.

1. Install Joomla.

---

[94] http://trends.builtwith.com/cms

[95] http://techcrunch.com/2011/06/11/joomla-quietly-crosses-23-million-downloads-now-powering-over-2600-government-sites/

[96] http://extensions.joomla.org/

2. <u>Create categories for your planned content</u>. The categories may be driven by your site map. For example, if you have a part of the site called About Us, you might create a corresponding category. Pages like Board of Directors, History, Mission and Vision, and Management would be included under this category.

3. Enter your content into the website using the Article Manager. Each planned page might become an article. Helpful resources for understanding this process include:

   3.1. <u>A Typical Article</u>

   3.2. <u>How to Create an 'About Us' Page</u>

   3.3. <u>Media Manager</u>, which is used for managing any images or documents you wish to include with your article

4. <u>Link articles to your navigation bars</u> on the website via the Menu Item Manager.

5. <u>Install a template</u> that makes the website look the way you wish. You can do this step earlier, but I find it easier to evaluate the look of a template once some content is available to me in the website.

6. <u>Configure any extensions</u> required for your website. For example, it's highly likely that you will want to <u>include a contact form</u> for your site.

7. Test your website carefully. Make sure the navigation links to the expected pages and functions on the site. Read all content carefully for typos. Look at the site in several different web browsers (like Firefox, Safari, Chrome, and Internet Explorer) on both Mac and PC platforms. The site does not need to be exactly the same, but it should look reasonable in all browsers.

8. Launch your website. You may wish to do a "soft launch" first, meaning you post the site without press releases or a big public promotion. This gives you some time to test the site in a real-world environment, while fixing any additional problems that may arise. Once the site has been active for a week or two, you can do a "hard launch", meaning creating publicity for the new site.

Chapter 22
Upgrade from older versions

UPDATE FROM JOOMLA 1.7

Well, that's an easy one.

Visit *Extensions → Extension Manager → Update*

click the button and your done!

It's the time to relax, grab a coffee and think:

> Well, it was a good decision to start my new project with Joomla 1.6/1.7

Attention: Many text strings in the language files are changed. The one-click update doesn't include local language packages. If you have installed local language packages it is necessary to update those, by reinstalling.

In case you think this 'one click solution' is far too easy. It cannot be true! Have a look at the more detailed Joomla documentation[97].

MIGRATE FROM JOOMLA 1.5

How can you migrate a Joomla 1.5 website to Joomla 2.5 without loss of data or similar disasters?

There are two ways to complete the update:

1. You can update the existing Joomla 1.5 website by using an additional component. This component loads all the necessary files with one click to your Joomla 1.5 website and automatically converts them to Joomla 2.5.

2. You can create an empty Joomla 2.5 website and insert the data from the Joomla 1.5 website manually.

Auto upgrade from Joomla 1.5 to Joomla 2.5

WARNING: The upgrade component I am using does not allow the transfer of data from **ALL** third-party components.

But, generally, I think the idea is a good one. :-)

Before you begin, please answer the following questions with a loud and clear YES.

---

[97] http://docs.joomla.org/Upgrade_1.6.5_to_1.7

Does your server environment meet the minimum requirements for Joomla 2.5?

- PHP, version 5.2.4 or higher

(**Not** for Joomla 1.7 but for the upgrade component, you will need the CURL module in PHP.)

- MySQL, version 5.0.4 or higher

Are all the installed extensions available for Joomla 2.5?

Have a look at the extension directory extensions[98].

Is the installed template available for Joomla 2.5, or are you able to change it manually?

Here is a good presentation by Chris Davenport[99]. It's about Joomla 1.6 but in general, nothing "important" changed in Joomla 2.5.

Are you experienced enough to change small snippets of code with instruction :-)?

If you feel comfortable and answered all the questions with yes ... let's go!

Step 1: Back-up

Before you do anything else, please do a backup of your site. You are probably already using *Akeeba Backup*[100]. If not, install it and do a back-up of your site!

Step 2: Create a local copy of your site

If you set up a local copy manually, you will need to

- copy your files
- dump your MySQL database, create a local database and import the dump into the local one
- change configuration.php

You can also implement the process with Akeeba backup, which allows you to create a zip package of your site. To again create a website from this package, you will need the *Akeeba Kickstarter*.[101]

- Place the kickstart files and the zip package of your website in the local folder of your website (*htdocs*).
- Create an empty database for your Joomla 1.5

---

[98] http://extensions.joomla.org/extensions/advanced-search-results/524478

[99] http://www.slideshare.net/chrisdavenport/template-changes-for-joomla-16

[100] http://extensions.joomla.org/extensions/access-a-security/site-security/backup/1606

[101] http://www.akeebabackup.com

- Launch kickstart.php. Presumably, the URL will look like http://localhost/kickstart.php. Then follow the instructions.

Step 3: Upgrade component

There is an upgrade component by Matias Aguirre[102]. The following data will be transfered:

It migrates for sure

- Banners - 100%
- Categories - 100%
- Contacts - 100%
- Content - 100%
- Menus - 100%
- Modules - 100%
- Newsfeeds - 100%
- Users - 100%
- Weblinks - 100%

Install the component[103] in your local Joomla 1.5 installation. Launch it and start the upgrade - that's it. :-)

The component creates a folder with the name jupgrade and installs the Joomla 1.7 variant of your 1.5 website in this new folder (http://localhost/jupgrade).

The Joomla 2.5 core template is activated..

Language files

If you use Joomla in a language other than English, you first have to install the correct language files[104].

Template

Customize your template and activate it.

GENERAL JOOMLA DEVELOPMENT STRATEGY

---

[102] http://twitter.com/maguirre

[103] http://redcomponent.com/jupgrade

[104] http://extensions.joomla.org/extensions/languages/translations-for-joomla

This wonderful graphic give you a precise idea of the future (*Figure 2*).

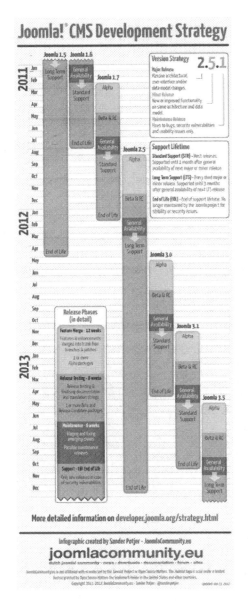

Figure 2: General Joomla Development Strategy (Graphic created by Sander Potjer[105])

---

[105] *http://sanderpotjer.nl/*

Chapter 23

written by Henk van Cann

Earning respect and money with Joomla

CMS implementation is difficult, but great to be involved with. How good you are technically, how socially connected your are, what a honest and hard worker you are - it doesn't add to the respect & money you receive.

This chapter deals with what you should and shouldn't do to make a living with Joomla implementation and support.

The things that do count in earning respect and money:

- be firm but sympathetic;
- Deadline first, flex the scope;
- Sell and negotiate continuously;
- Define roles and play them!

WHY ME?

Do you ever:

- have customers that don't pay your invoice?
- work twice as much as you're getting paid for?
- have a big misunderstanding about the deliverables with your customer?
- encounter disrespectful behavior of clients?
- frown upon the choices customers make in your field of expertise?
- get no or low appreciation for what you've delivered?
- need to battle scope creep?
- take much longer to deliver, but the customer did not care?

- discuss with your partner wife or husband about whether it's a good idea to continue your firm
- think of going back to a normal and easy job?

You are not alone.

If all the answers are 'no' you are natural talent in earning respect & money with open source CMS expertise.

Or you've worked through this chapter before?

DENIAL

After years of long days and hard work, you only find your soul mates at open source congresses and meetings. Where we share our experiences. Or via the IRC channel, where we like to complain about our customers: they're stupid, they don't want to pay, they think they know it all, they expect you to go to work without them putting pen to paper, and so on.

What's happening here is that we are in denial. The customer is not the problem. We ourselves have to change our attitude.

"I'm not good at selling, I like to build systems."

Fair enough, but did you start up your own organization to be in charity work? Charity workers get respect and "sell" their free help.

If you have decided to start your own firm, not selling is not an option. You have to get off the wrong bus quickly.

"I'm not what you call a salesperson - I'm too soft. To be honest: I hate selling."

You need a change in how you perceive the world. Selling is a profession that should be indicated as "assisting with purchasing". Put aside your prejudice! Start assisting your customer in purchasing the right things (instead of selling), and teach them how to give you the respect and treatment you deserve, plus payment.

"Larger organizations don't contract small firms on their bigger projects."

Play their game, play it well and they will hire you.

"My customers don't work this way."

Well, then get a different type of customer, or teach your current customers "how it works".

"There is not much money to be made in open source"

On the contrary: Open source integration has at least five major innovational effects[106] that closed source can't beat. Proven and indisputable. For that reason long term or short term replacement propositions of closed source by open source "are" big money. Just because closed source is about big money. Closed source will eventually adapt itself to open source innovation. But that will take time. In the meanwhile, your expertise is worth respect & money. If your have not been convinced yet, click the link above about the said innovative effects of open technology because you need to ooze pride.

Still in denial?

Sorry for bothering you! Please continue your good work and put your mind at rest with the other chapters you'll find in this book. One last request: could you please efface yourself quietly, poor and lonely? :-)

The other chapters are very much worth reading. Don't get me wrong. Don't however lull yourself to sleep by obtaining more technical knowledge only as a distraction from a totally different ballgame: earning respect & money. Because that's got nothing to do with Joomla, Drupal, TYPO3 or any other world class open source CMS, nor your great expertise.

Awake? Good, we need a clear mind to learn & practice how to earn respect & money with our expertise & means.

THREE THING YOU NEED TO BE AWARE OF ALL THE WAY THROUGH

- Your reputation
- Your role(s)
- Your task(s)

Add a. Your reputation

In general, the reputation of IT workers can be found at the low end of the spectrum of respected jobs. Not sure you agree? Try it!

1. Wear a suit, start talking of a business proposition to anybody. Suddenly switch to the details of a possible IT-implementation of that particular proposition. Your credibility decreases instantly.

2. Mention your IT-profession at a party to (female) young urban professionals. Just look at the faces.

Add b&c. Your roles and tasks

In organizations, our IT-job is to persist in constant expectation management, infinite selling and sticking to plans

---

[106] http://www.2value.nl/en/weblog/weblog/five-innovative-characteristics-of-open-source

The good news is that there is a lot of material available detailing the process of a web system implementation. The bad news: help, humans are involved!

Problems are those weird things that pop up when you don't have your eye on the ball: earn money and respect.

FIRST SOME DEFINITIONS
Resource
A resource is pending input from a customer or third party. If you don't get the resource, you can't do or finish your job. E.g. digital photos from a photographer, a list of menu-item names in a different language, a signature on the contract of your assignment (oops, you never ask for that?), etc.

Resourceplanning
Ensuring that the input of customers and third parties is ready for use in a project or support.

Scope
The extent of a solution. The size and magnitude of an effort, expertise, machinery, functionality that is wanted/planned to offer that solution. <google scope - wikipedia>

Functionality-blocks
A logical group of functionality under a common title. Expressed in normal "homo sapiens" language. E.g. a forum, design, interface, advanced search. (A homo digitalis would invent titles like Jomsocial, psd plus html/css and template based on wire frame, database lookup of indexed content.)

Release plan
The release plan specifies which Functionality-blocks are going to be implemented for each system release and dates for those releases. The release plan specifies who (in which role) fulfills the particular tasks.

Sprint
All efforts within a certain phase in a project (as agreed in a release plan). The word "sprint" suggests running to a deadline, no time to lose. We have to catch an airplane in time. Because the airplane will leave and we better be on it. And therefore we might not pack our bag that well, some items might be missing, we might go in fits and starts, but we get there in time! By doing so, we are much better off than having all stuff beautifully packed: everything we might need is packed in the suitcase, but we are left behind on the airport.

SprintX
The virtual sprint after the last planned sprint within the release plan. It is a container for extra work (scope creep or agreed out of scope) or waiting area for functionality-blocks that couldn't be implemented in the sprints so far.

Contract management

The management of contracts made with customers, vendors, partners, or employees. Contract management includes negotiating the terms and conditions in contracts and ensuring compliance with the terms and conditions, as well as documenting and agreeing on any changes that may arise during its implementation. The purpose: maximizing financial and operational performance and minimizing risk.

Project management

The discipline of planning, organizing, securing and managing resources to bring about the successful completion of specific project goals and objectives. Put it differently: running from A to B without looking up and getting there in time; no matter what.

Findings

How people perceive the world and in an open source web system / Joomla implementation in particular: how people see results in the context of what is agreed. We need to elaborate on Findings a bit more because synchronization of Findings is the key to a valuable contract management.

FINDINGS

Findings are complex. We might have conflicting interests, personal issues versus the roles we play. Different levels of expertise and experience. How well were negotiations perceived. What about respect? Did parties involved that wrote their Findings receive enough respect from others and give enough respect to others during the process? All these factors influence the way we perceive things.

Example: An emotional quarrel with your neighbor hardly ever has to do with the subject or object at hand. Most likely it's something else that formed their opinion, expressed in a sort of "Findings".

HOUSEHOLD PSYCHOLOGY ONE-ON-ONE

Let's also have a quick look at some important psychological effects while doing business. In case of an open source web system implementation, we stumble upon a few interesting effects that have a major impact.

What a customer really wants

Cover and future proof advice. That is it, folks. He/she is not interested in open source, Joomla, you, your product, your measures, your vision, etc. So stop telling them dumb stories and start asking smart questions to secure them in what they really want.

The declining value of service

Everything that is already done, is worth less every following day and everything that needs to be done is very important and urgent. Does it ring a bell?

Always right

A customer is always right. If not, we just have a different opinion on the subject... That is a good example of what synchronization of Findings is all about.

DEADLINE FIRST FLEX SCOPE

Projects tend to go over the deadline. Why? Are you such a crappy planner, do you like to disappoint people? Of course not. Do you end up with a buggy result to has to be debugged, do you accept new requirements and changed resources while you are developing? Yes, you do. Do you have a problem stopping development efforts and starting a thorough test? Do you deliver half-baked systems just to "keep the customer happy"? You most probably do. And you should stop this behavior from this moment on.

"Deadline first" means: no matter what, we deliver on time. Read that sentence again: we deliver on time.

40 years of ICT has done us no good in some perspectives. It's perfectly accepted that we don't deliver on time. Even worse: it's accepted that more than 50% of the larger ICT projects world wide are a sheer failure. And we accept that they tend to be twice as expensive in the end than quoted upfront.

Suppose your grocery store would say "no milk today" after you ordered it by phone yesterday. Suppose your bakery would raise their prices from one day to the other by 100% or 200%. What would you say if the constructor of your house that just collapsed sends you the last invoice for "work done to your house"?

Customers in ICT just walk off and mumble their disdain. They go and start another ICT project. And we suppliers? We get away with nonperformance! We don't deliver on time, we don't stick to promises and we deliver systems that will not be used (long enough). Sometimes a customer sues us. But what the hack: you can't get blood from a stone. In many cases, angry customers don't pay the last installment or the main installment (depends on how stupid we were). But that's about it. Easy walk in the park. We continue to next project and act more or less the same...

STOP IT!

Deliver on time, no matter what, no excuses, but deliver!

HOW TO DELIVER ON TIME

I will now go into detail about how it's done and the positive effects of this behavior for all parties involved, including your customers.

How do you deliver on time?
Most importantly by flexing the scope.

The Basecamp-company 37signals[107] writes in their visionary guidebook *Getting Real*[108]: open source (and also Joomla) web systems are very well equipped to stick to this rule. (Read the full book for other good rules)

1. Open source has good prototyping & Proof of Concept capabilities, scope gets clearer "after" prototyping and thus scope changes.

2. An Open source web system has extensive and useful hidden functionality on board, loads of change available (see also Negotiate continuously)

3. Scope should be flexible because customers change their mind on what they want, after experiencing first results and possibilities. Customers learn on the job. And change their mind accordingly. Scope creep is the negative effect, "flex scope" the positive solution.

This is the step-by-step:

Agree upfront that you put deadline first and flex the scope to meet the deadline. Explain honestly what "flex scope" means. Lets call the customers "they". Be very open: what they want now, they don't get in the end. Why not? Why not? Advancing insight will eventually lead to different systems! However they do get what they want in every iteration towards the end result.

Be sure to be in charge of flexing the scope (no discussion, you have to meet the deadline, so you're the one that makes decisions after touching base.

Plan a time buffer in your work towards a deadline. Use the buffer to flex the scope and make an new version of your release plan. Do that by diminishing the number of functionality-blocks in the current sprint, slim down functionality-blocks.

Manage possible frustration of customers

Never write off a functionality block yourself. Place it in a next sprint or in SprintX.

Communicate the flex scope action with a new Release plan

Stick to priorities in the Findings so far and write down every single remark (no duplicates) or new wish explicitly.

BE FIRM BUT SYMPATHETIC

Main firm stands:

1. Never ever accept a fixed price contract again. Or make a ridiculous margin on top of your quote. Open source web system development and implementation is just not suited to offer and work

---

[107] http://37signals.com/

[108] http://gettingreal.37signals.com/

with a fixed price. Explore 2Value's alert system[109] as a balanced alternative in between fixed price and "Carte Blanche".

2. Stick to the rules of engagement: payments overdue? Stop work right away, no exceptions.

3. Professionalism: start to offer it by demanding it.

Sympathetic behavior accompanied with a firm stand

1. A: Always say and write: We "can't" instead of "we don't want to" or "we won't".

Example: I am sorry sir, I am afraid I can't continue staging your site to production. The partial payment has not arrived in our bank account. It's company policy to proceed only if due payments have arrived in our bank account.

2. B: Say you can't start this server virus-fix analysis before the money has arrived in the bank account, but let the customer "feel" that your back office has already taken measures and is full on the job of analyzing & fixing the bug.

3. C: A support contract is hardly ever a result insurance. Support on webCMS's, especially those based on open source can only be a guided effort insurance. That means: at the most we promise reaction, response and resolve times and capacity available in the required expertise.

Don't introduce this result responsibility of customers site on your business' shoulder. They can't bear it. The load of several million lines of code… someone else's code. Code running on a contentiously changing stack that's attacked by scoundrels every day (hackers).

> Remember: Before the customer first rang your door bell, their site was never your problem. Keep that in mind and remind your customer. Some of these customers think they can buy your commitment, devotion, hiring you as a templater for a few hours…. And some of you act like sinners right away when a customer is in great distress and quick to point the finger at you because of a non-operating web system. Again: behave like a professional and they will respect you as a professional. Behave like a low grade assistant, they will treat you as a doormat.

A webCMS is the customers problem and we can assist by improving it and helping out when problems occur. It is not your problem. Comprendo? Tiny difference, huge effect. Only watch the tone of voice.

Having said (and repeated) that, you work your ass off to help this customers web shop to go live again before the rush of Christmas shopping.

- D: We do deliver exactly what was agreed (no rebate for nothing), but we "put in the extra mile" too.

---

[109] http://wiki.2value.nl/index.php?title=Piepsysteem/en

Sell and negotiate continuously

It's obvious that you have to sell a project and negotiate conditions (among them "price"). What is new to many people is that in a web system development project or the support afterwards, you have to sell and negotiate continuously.

A few examples:

- Is it done? Can I send my invoice now? ("No, there is still a few issues left to improve…")

- Support request: change a logo on the site. How much time do you need? ("Ooh, come on you can't be serious!…")

- You think it is extra work, your customer doesn't seem to think so. ("It might not be in the RFP, but I remember very well us discussing this functionality")

Remember that sales is game. The customer should have the overall feeling that he/she won that game. Give them that feeling and be well-off with the deal at the same time!

To be able to play a game of marbles, you'll need marbles.

How do you get marbles? By signing the contract? No. By sending invoices? No no. By holding back results. Sometimes…

The main source of credits for your sales game are happiness and money. Don't mix them.

- Build up credits in the emotional bank account of your relations (See Steven R. Covey[110]). Solve frustration you might have; you need to be happy in the work relation too!

- If partial payments have arrived on time, you have credits for new games.

- Refrain from having too many service hours unpaid. It makes you vulnerable and clears the way for customers to put you under pressure and/or reopen negotiations. The more they owe you, the more they might throw in these bullshit arguments to not proceed and pay you. Inappropriate pressure is coming down on you. But you caused it yourself in the first place. (See: be firm but sympathetic)

Define roles and play them!

A customer has several broadly accepted roles: the boss, the end user, the administrator of the web system, and most important he/she is the judge.

As a literal 'sole' proprietary holder you stand alone as the supplier of the web system. You have to deliver the system: good, suitable, well documented, within time, within budget en reliable. How fair is that?

Well, that's not fair at all! Lets have a closer look at what is happening here.

---

[110] http://en.wikipedia.org/wiki/Stephen_Covey

Suppose you ooze that "do it all and liking it" attitude. You get questions like:

> "Would you advice us to use Joomla?"

and

> "Could PHP do the backup cycle for us"

and

> "Is it possible to get multilingual support in time?".

Nothing wrong with these questions, right? How often did you answer them?…without realizing that you just loaded the barrels of a shotgun pointed at you.

Suppose you answer these questions with "Yes", and refined the answer. That's very nice of you! You know a lot! The respect you get originates from the fact that you're not only a good developer, but also:

- have a very sharp vision on how the selection process should be;
- feel acquainted and safe with the LAMP stack and cronjob-mechanism and you fix it (woow!)
- that the international open source community and especially a web CMS Joomla is a sort of homecoming for you; you know a lot of people, anywhere in the world….

> 'What a man, what a man, what a talented man.

No idea where we're heading? Hold on and "no worries", these are just harmless examples to get you to understand the risks of being foolishly responsive.

Lets pull the trigger of the shotgun pointed at you. Remember that it was you that loaded the ammunition:

- Now wait a minute, you advised Joomla and now we have to program tailor-made code that might solve the issue that Drupal does out of the box?!…'
- Every night we expected to have a safe copy of our website, because you said PHP was capable of doing it. We paid you to configure the cronjob. And now we ended up with a useless restore…"
- You promised multilingual support and now we have to pay for it?'

Where did the respect go that you counted on? Why does this customer behave like this? It's obvious that the customer is angry and I guess you have to work for free to make her or him happy again! So what's your best bet, pal?

What went wrong? A few elementary things in conducting professional business. And please don't lull yourself to sleep with

> oh, no but I'm just a small firm, a creative entrepreneur, and my customers are small. I do not need this.

Joomla! 2.5 - Beginner's Guide

A few elementary and universal things in conducting professional business went wrong:

- You didn't separate your different talents in distinctive roles. Symbolize them by different colored caps. So from now on: define roles.

- You didn't put on the right caps while answering the questions. That made you vulnerable: the customer can take your answer from any point of view. Play your role!

HOW DO YOU DEFINE ROLES?

You don't have to. Definitions are readily available, just choose a set of roles that match your business and communicate them. Put them in writing and make your customer acquainted with the various roles you play professionally. Examples: account manager, consultant, contract manager, project manager, designer, developer, tester, content-builder, hoster.

A customer or its representative will only abuse you playing 10 roles at a time IF YOU ALLOW THEM TO.

To be safe and sound. Use these roles explicitly at all important times and play them.

> I am sorry, ms. customer, as your developer I could never answer your "should we use Joomla" question. The reason is your organization has to choose a webCMS and I can make the best of it. Of course I can connect you with mr. colleague_of_mine, he is consultant at our company and specialized in selection-processes. His fee is very reasonable compared to the coverage of corporate risks he covers with his advice.
>
> PHP for the backup cycle. As a contract manager I would have to say 'no' to you, because a backup procedure is out of scope. As a project manager I'm afraid I have to give you the same answer for a different reason: we are busy in this sprint reaching the deadline, we haven't planned it and I don't have the backup routine in the release plan as a listed functionality that I have to fulfill. As a developer I would say: yes, doable. But the alarm bells go off in my office as a hoster: first the characteristics of the restore should be clear before we could invent a suitable back-up strategy. You see, there are many ways of looking at this simple question.
>
> Multilingual support in time? You have to be more specific to avoid disappointment in the near future. I could say Yes to you, because it's easy to install a translation module. That's my development cap. But somebody has got to do the translations as well. And that could be me in a different role, different cap: translator/configurator. If you expect 'Multilingual support' to be localized content, I would have to perform a task that I am not able to: I am not a native speaker of the foreign language that you focus at and I'm not a citizen that lives locally in that region. Whether or not I can perform the tasks in time that I am

capable of doing, depends on the planning. I have to take a look at that next Thursday when I have my project management-day.

This all might seem a silly play, but it is dead serious business.

Tactics
Example: interaction design

Your tomorrow's user interaction design session with the customer will be easier if someone else (but on behalf of you) mentioned the cascade of your legal steps against him, as long as invoices remain unpaid. You could tap the customer's arm and say "please do not be to angry on him, he just doing his job. We can not blame him, can we?" The customer will respect him for his and yours professionalism. Image how hard it is to play these roles all by yourself.

- To avoid backfire on your personal relationship with your customer you could "'introduce your real colleagues'" (individuals). Real colleagues (even if they do not know that they are your colleague) are very good to have around, you can:
    - a. blame them
    - b. praise them for their excellent work in his/hers role
- To postpone and divert: answer the question in one or two roles right away, but then park as an agenda-item for a different role on the critical path. Example given: "Yes, technically no problem, but I have to take a look at that next Thursday when I have my project management-day."
- Invent a diversion yourself. It's nothing to be ashamed of. In business it is done every day. Ask yourself the question "Does it sound as an excuse?" It shouldn't. It should be a "role well played".

Revisited

The 4 interdependent rules of earning respect and money in your work as an open source expert revisited:

- Deadline first, flex scope
- Be firm but sympathetic
- Sell en negotiate continuously
- Define roles and play them

See?!: **Earning respect and money with Joomla has nothing to do with Joomla.**

(Thanks to Froukje Frijlink who checked my English).

Chapter 24
Resources

This book was a beginning. I hope you enjoyed reading it. My intention was to guide you through Joomla 2.5. Not everything was covered because that would have been too much.

I think we could use a developer book and a template designer book to dip deeper into these topics. Nobody knows what the future holds in store!

What kind of useful resources are there for you to learn more about Joomla or to get in touch with the Joomla community?

COMMUNITY

As it is written on the back of this book, Joomla is backed by a worldwide community. If you like this idea, come and join us!

- Become a member of http://community.joomla.org/.

- Read the community magazine at http://magazine.joomla.org/.

- Maybe there is a Joomla user group near you that you can join.
  http://community.joomla.org/user-groups.html
  If not, start one yourself!

- Twitter: http://twitter.com/joomla

- Facebook Group: http://www.facebook.com/joomla

DOCUMENTATION
- http://docs.joomla.org/

SECURITY CHECKLIST
- http://docs.joomla.org/Security_Checklist_1_-_Getting_Started

JOOMLA EXTENSIONS
- The Joomla extension directory provides more than 8,888 extensions - http://extensions.joomla.org/

JOOMLA TEMPLATES
- There is no central directory for free templates.

- There is no central directory for commercial templates.

Anyway, there are a lot of template clubs and professionals that provide Joomla templates. Just search the web and you will most certainly find something that suits you.

EVENTS

- Joomla is known for its Joomla days.
- A Joomla day is a one- or two-day event organized by and for the community. A list of Joomla days can be found here http://community.joomla.org/events.htm
- There is an international Joomla conference in Europe called *jandbeyond*. Go to http://jandbeyond.org/ for more information.
- In November 2012 there will be the first Joomla world conference (San Jose)

Date: 16th-18th November 2012
Location:
eBay Town Hall
2161 North First Street
San Jose, CA 95131
USA

THE FUTURE

- The community plans a six month release cycle, based on the ideas people post in the Joomla idea pool.
- The next long term release will be Joomla 3.5 in May 2013
- The Joomla developer network is always looking for people like you :-) http://developer.joomla.org/

TRAINING

- http://resources.joomla.org/directory/support-services/training.html

COMMERCIAL SUPPORT

- http://resources.joomla.org/

HOSTING

- http://resources.joomla.org/directory/support-services/hosting.html

CERTIFICATES

At the moment there is no possibility to get certified in Joomla.

You see, there is enough work left for you, your friends and the rest of the world :-).

cocoate

www.cocoate.com

cocoate.com

is the publisher of this book and an independent management consultancy, based in France and working internationally.

Specialised in three areas – Consulting, Coaching and Teaching – cocoate.com develops web based strategies for process and project management and public relations; provides customized trainings for open source content management systems Drupal, Joomla and WordPress, in the area of management and leadership skills and develops educational projects with the focus on non-formal learning.

The European educational projects focus on the promotion of lifelong learning with the goal of social integration. Particular emphasis is placed on learning methods in order to learn how to learn, the conception and realization of cross-generational learning strategies and local community development.

http://cocoate.com

Made in the USA
Lexington, KY
24 October 2016